Understanding the Jewish World

From Roman to Byzantine Times

Mishnah • Talmud • The Sages
An Introductory Atlas

MICHAEL AVI-YONAH

•

SHMUEL SAFRAI

cartaJerusalem

First published in 2015 by
CARTA Jerusalem

18 Ha'uman Street, P.O.B. 2500,
Jerusalem 9102401, Israel
E-mail: carta@carta.co.il
www.carta-jerusalem.com

Cartography: Carta, Jerusalem

Adapted from: Carta's Atlas of the Period of the Second Temple:
The Mishnah and the Talmud © Carta 1966; 1974
Historical Atlas of the Jewish People © Carta 2003
Illustrations added for this edition.

Picture Sources
Pictures are via Wikimedia Commons, and have been attributed to their authors.
All other illustrations are from the archives of Carta, Jerusalem

Map: *The Sages of Jabneh*: redacted by Zeev Safrai.

Great care has been taken to establish sources of illustrations. If inadvertently we failed to do so, due credit will be given in the next edition.

ISBN: 978-965-220-867-5

Printed in the United States of America

CONTENTS

INTRODUCTION

The land of Israel has been a battleground since time immemorial and the first century CE was no exception. The most disastrous event for the Jewish people was the destruction of their Holy Temple on the 9th of Av in 70 CE. That, according to tradition, was the very same day that the First Temple had been destroyed centuries earlier. The loss of the Temple was not the only traumatic event. A great many wars, campaigns and rebellions, often followed by destruction and massacres or exile, occurred at the time, culminating in the Bar Kokhba revolt.

This book attempts to address and depict the effect these upheavals had for the next half-century on the history of the Jewish people, how they carried on their lives and kept performing their often severely restricted, religious observances under new circumstances. Daily life and spiritual development are duly chronicled; much attention is given to the generations of sages who created the Mishnah and the Talmud in the Land of Israel and Babylonia.

Notably, the onset of the first century witnessed also the birth, deeds and martyrdom of Jesus and the acts of his apostles. The sometime divergence from established tradition led to the emergence of Christianity, a new faith that was fast becoming the dominant religion of the western world and incidentally brought with it a new calendar—BC/AD or BCE/CE, now in its third millennium.

Transportation and Economy in the Roman Empire

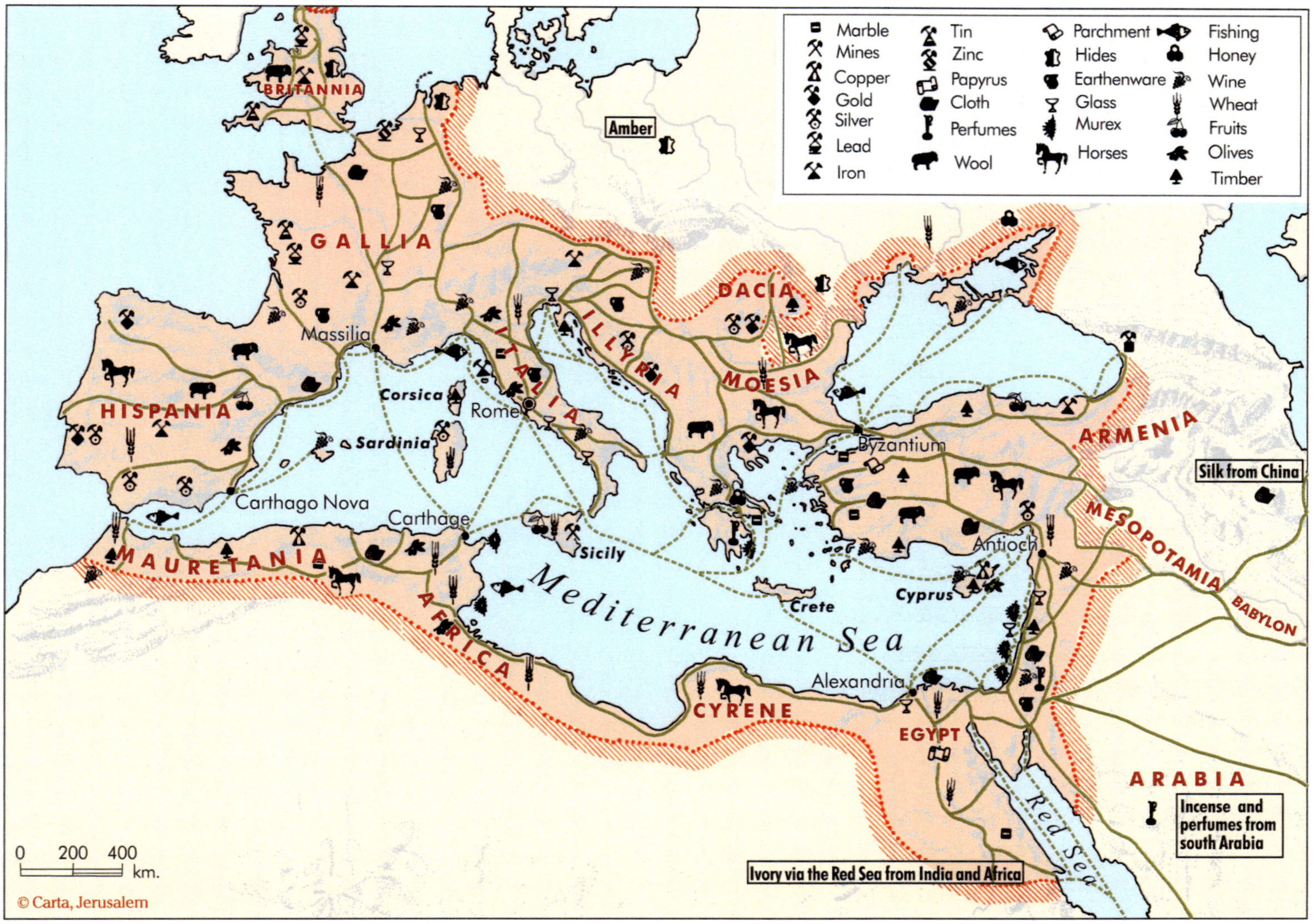

The Roman conquest of Eretz Israel in particular and of the Mediterranean lands as a whole caused the Jewish inhabitants of the former, and even more so the Diaspora Jews, to integrate within the economic framework of the Mediterranean Basin. This region for the first time was consolidated under one rule. At the start of their Empire, the Romans ruled the Hellenistic nations of the East, including their industrial centers, along with many countries in the West. These latter were only partially developed, if at all, but were rich in raw materials needed for the industries of Italy and the East. In Italy proper, industrialization grew, based on eastern know-how. In the first two centuries of the Common Era, the natural resources of the northern and western provinces of the Empire, e.g., the iron mines in the Alps and in Gallia were developed, and especially those in the west and south of Spain – the richest of all in various metals. Following the conquest of Britannia by Claudius, the iron and tin of this distant island also became available.

In the eastern part of the Empire, the economic development did not undergo particular changes, but the cessation of wars freed trade and industry from many obstacles. Only in the field of agriculture did the Romans strengthen their conservative base. In the time of Augustus, some of the new innovations and discoveries of the late Hellenistic period, such as glass-blowing, came into use. In this industry, Jews from Phoenicia and the Land of Israel played an important role. The discovery of their ability to exploit monsoon winds by Alexandrian merchants in the late Hellenistic period, promoted trade with India. Clay and silver vessels, as well as Roman coins, were able to reach India, while in return, perfumes, spices, fabrics, silk and other luxury commodities arrived from India to the ports of Aila (Elath) and the port city of Clysma (Suez). Italy itself, the center of power and rule, prospered in the first century when the provinces could furnish their industries with raw materials. Moreover, Egypt, Africa and Asia Minor supplied wheat, oil and wine for the citizens of Rome. From the East, luxury items became available for the estates of senators and the aristocracy.

However, in the Antonine period (96–180 CE), a change occurred in the economic structure of the Empire. The proprietors of the industries left Italy and established new centers in the western provinces of the Empire. Thus, for example, the manufacture of *terra sigillata* ware which had been centred in Arretium, now began to prosper in Gallia and Germania. This is only one example of many such instances.

The road network of the Empire also promoted the spread of industry away from its center in Italy. The relative decline of Italy created an economic and political "hole" in the center of the Empire. This process endangered the welfare of Rome and finally caused the severe crisis that befell the empire in the third century.

Christians and Jews in Eretz Israel
After the Revolt Against the Romans – First Century CE

Although the war of CE 66 to 70 was fierce both in Galilee and in Judea — and especially in Jerusalem and a few other places where the fighting was particularly severe — the Jewish population in general remained intact; many lands did, however, pass from Jewish to imperial possession. The evidence of the revolt of Bar Kokhba is in itself enough to show that Judea was still settled with Jews at the beginning of the second century. The persistence of Judaism in Galilee in later centuries shows the same trend. After the destruction of the Temple and the uprooting of the leading classes, some Jews did remain in Jerusalem. The reconstituted Sanhedrin at Jamnia (Jabneh) extended its authority over the nation.

The disasters of the Jewish War seem to have caused an estrangement between the Jews and the Judeo-Christians. The Jerusalem community of Christians had left the Holy City on the eve of the siege, taking refuge at Pella beyond the Jordan. Some of its members later returned to continue in Jerusalem; others stayed behind. The communities founded by the Apostles in the coastal plain survived, as did some of the Judeo-Christian groups at Capernaum, Kefar-schania (Sachnin) in Galilee and Cochaba in the Galilee or Syria, and some other places. However, there is little evidence of the thousands of converts mentioned in early sources. The breach with Judaism was not yet formal, though the traditional constancy of most of the Jews, along with other factors, turned the efforts of the Christian missionaries more and more toward the Gentiles in the Holy Land and abroad.

The Tabernacle as represented in the synagogue at Capernaum

AFTERMATH OF THE BAR KOKHBA REVOLT:

The Decrees of Hadrian 135 CE

We are sure that within a few days there will not be a place in the whole of Palestine where corpses of the people will not be laying about.

Tractate *Semahot* ch.8

With the suppression of the Revolt a period of persecutions began, which Jewish sources term "the Religious Persecution" (*Ha-Shmad*). The plan of the Roman government was to completely eradicate all Jewish settlement in Judea and to blur the Jews' national identity in the rest of the land. Hadrian ordered the expulsion of all Jews who remained in Judea, thus emptying the region of most of its inhabitants. When the battles began, many Jews had already escaped, to such a degree that the Mediterranean ports were crowded with refugees. Those who were taken prisoner by the Roman army were sold in two large slave markets, one in Botana (north of Hebron) and the other in Gaza. The number of prisoners-of-war was so large that the price of slaves decreased in all the markets of the empire. Hadrian ensured the reinstatement of Aelia Capitolina (Jerusalem) and settled the city and its environs with foreigners, mainly Arabians and Syrians. Entry to the city was forbidden to the circumcised, including Christians of Jewish origin.

Judea was left with only rural settlements, in "Daroma" ("the South"), from En-gedi to Gerar, in the lowlands of Jamnia and Lydda, and in the Jordan Valley, from En-gedi to Livias. From this time forth, the Galilee became the main refuge of Palestinian Jewry. But even there a foreign image was imposed on the city councils of Tiberias and Sepphoris, the latter city being renamed "Diocaesarea." Hadrian aspired to destroy all memory of the defeated people and ordered that the name of Judea be changed to "Syria Palaestina."

The leaders who had supported Bar Kokhba were put to death. Among them were the "Ten Martyrs," headed by Rabbi Akiva, who died a martyr's death in Caesarea. R. Yeshevav the Scribe and R. Huzpit ha-Meturgeman ("the Translator") apparently fled to Sepphoris, but the authorities caught up with them there, as they did with R. Hananiah b. Teradyon, in Sogane. To weaken the Jews' self-image, the Romans forbade the performance of numerous commandments such as circumcision, and congregating in the synagogue. The Romans also prohibited rabbinical ordination, i.e., passing full judicial authority from one generation of sages to another. The authorities threatened to destroy any town which tolerated this practice. Nonetheless, R. Judah b. Bava martyred himself by ordaining five students of R. Akiva between Shepharam and Usha, thereby ensuring the continuation of this judicial system. Many sages of this generation, such as R. Simeon bar Yohai, went into hiding. Others, like R. Meir and R. Yose, fled the country for a time. Nevertheless, the existence of a Diaspora Jewry that remained scattered in places either unaffected or outside the boundaries of the empire, nullified Hadrian's decrees to some extent.

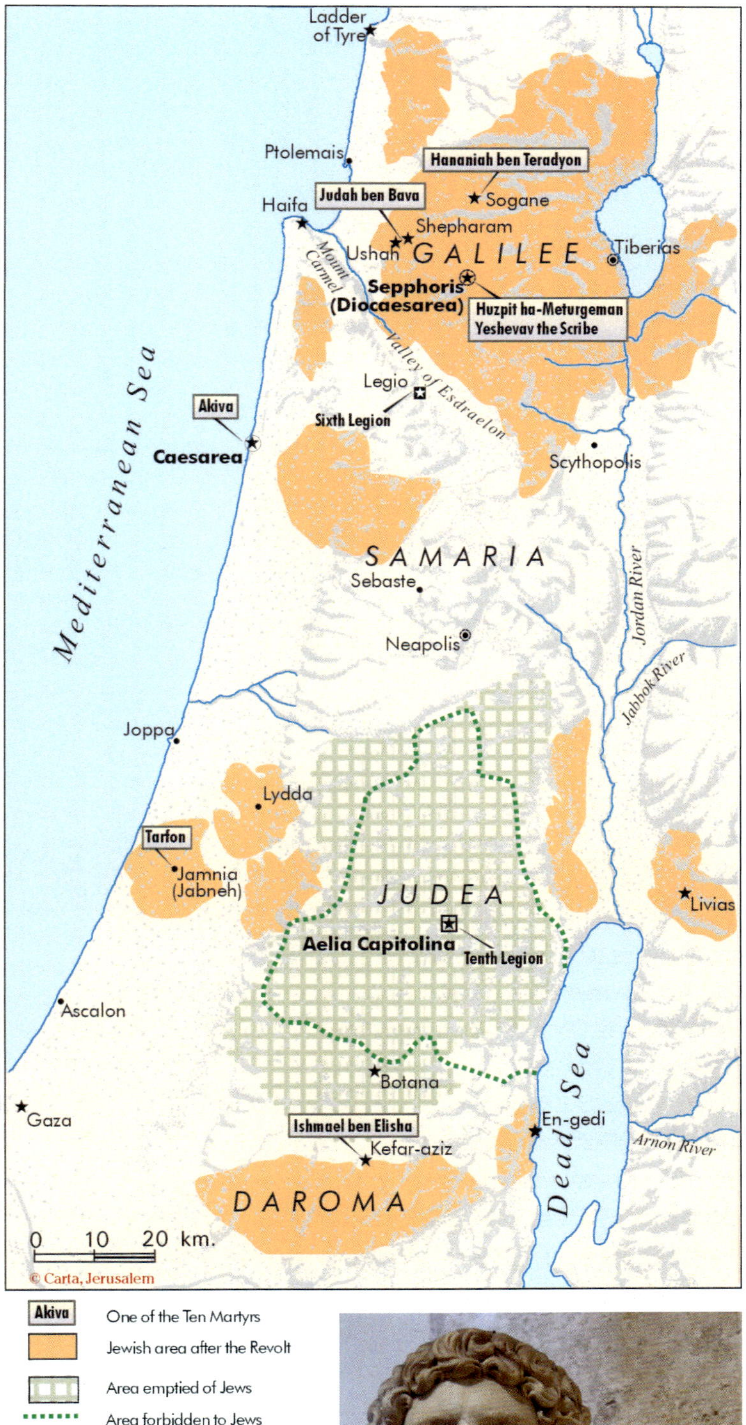

Bust of Hadrian; Capitoline Museum (photo: Marie Lan Nguyen).

The Sages of Jabneh

In the wake of the traumatic destruction of Jerusalem and its Temple, the spiritual life of the nation was rescued through the charismatic personality of Rabban Johanan ben Zakkai. It is unclear whether he had opposed the revolt; but he had cautioned the rebels against over-confidence: "Do not haste to tear down altars of Gentiles, lest you be forced to rebuild them with your own hands, lest you tear down altars of bricks and be ordered to build them of stone" (Avot of Rabbi Nathan, Version B 31). According to local tradition Johanan approached Vespasian and his son Titus and sought their permission, "to perform commandments and teach Torah" at Jabneh. Thus, he began to rebuild Jewish spiritual life in the void left by the destruction of the Temple. He reconvened the Sanhedrin and began to establish the New Moons at Jabneh.

Rabban Gamaliel succeeded Johanan at the end of the Flavian dynasty. Under his authority the national leadership at Jabneh was given *de jure* recognition by Rome.

Not only did the Sanhedrin at Jabneh attain imperial recognition, it also won the acknowledgment from wide Jewish circles in the Land of Israel and the Diaspora. The authority of the Sanhedrin in Jabneh was now established, and the communal and spiritual life of the nation was in the hands of the Torah scholars, who were distinguished by ordination from their peers and who now bore the designation "rabbi."

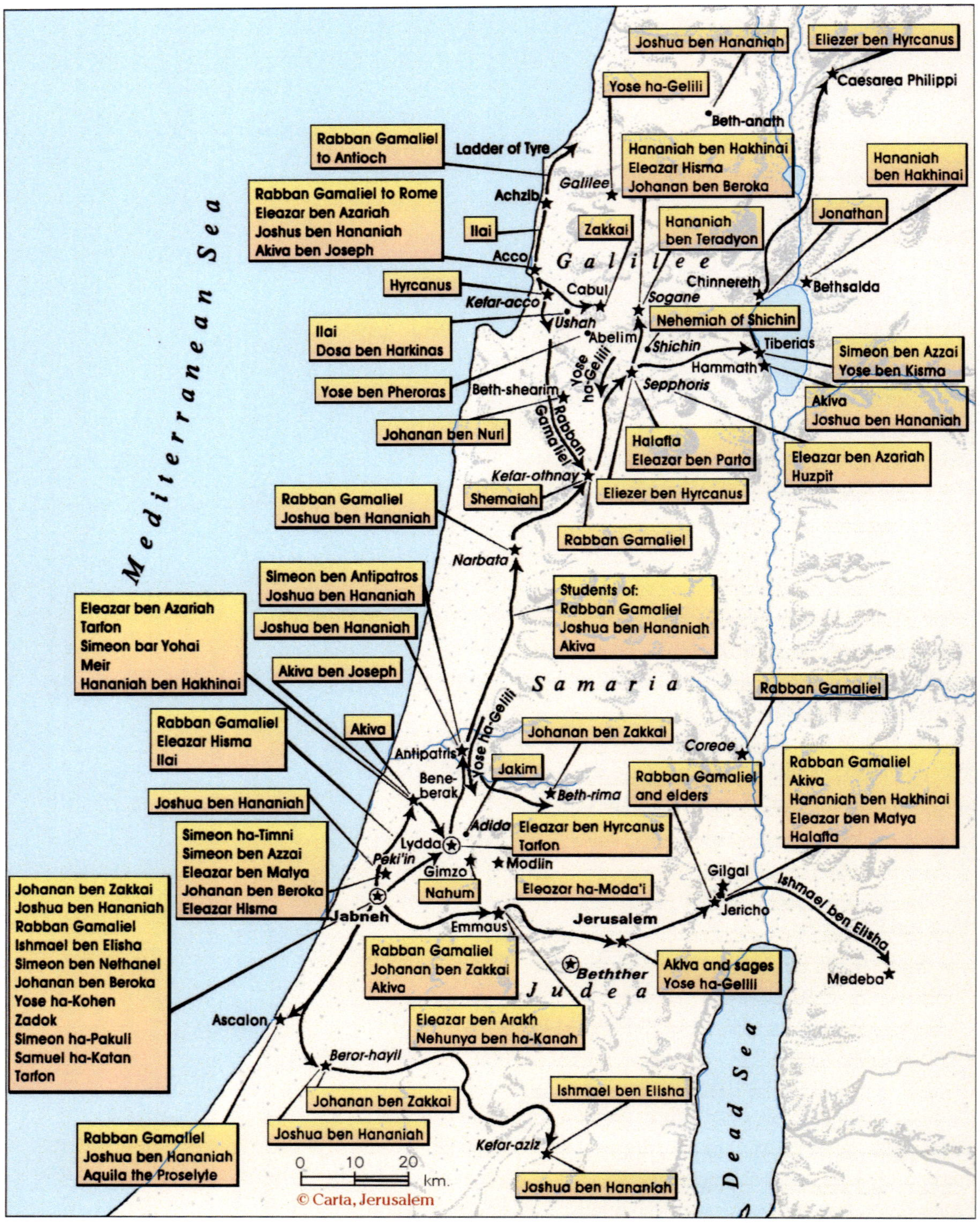

Tomb of Rabban Gamliel inYavneh (Jabneh) (photo: Avishai Teicher)

The Boundaries of the Land According to *Halakhah*

Talmudic sources distinguish three borders of Eretz Israel: "the boundary of the Patriarchs," from the river of Egypt (the Nile) to the river Euphrates; "the boundary of those coming out of Egypt," that is, the borders of Joshua's conquests; and "the boundary of those returning from Babylonia." Unlike the first two, which are mainly of historical significance, the third "boundary" had halakhic and practical significance. This boundary generally separated those Jewish settlements that were considered part of Eretz Israel and which were subject to halakhic rules relating to the land—such as *terumot* (heave offerings), tithes, and the prohibition of planting and harvesting in the seventh, or Sabbatical year (*shevi'it*)—from other areas that, halakhically speaking, were "land of the Gentiles."

The "boundary of those returning from Babylonia" is listed in three versions: in *Sifrei* (*Ekev*, v. 51), and in *Shevi'it* of both the Tosefta (4:11) and the Jerusalem Talmud (4:36c). These accounts are faulty with regard to many names and to the order in which they are arranged. After making various corrections and changes of order, we arrive at the line depicted on the map. Along the coast, cities considered Gentile were excluded from the Land of Israel: Ascalon (from "the junction," namely, where the Ascalon road intersects the coastal road, a place identified with "Ganei Ashkelon," where the list ends); Caesarea (listed under its old name, Strato's Tower, distorted here to "Sharshon's Tower"); Dora and Acco. From Acco the border continued along the northbound road, to the left (west) of which was the "land of the Gentiles" and to the right (east), the Land of Israel. The boundary passed near several settlements within the townships of Acco and Tyre, and turned northeastward, up to the Ijon Valley, between the Lebanon and Hermon mountain ranges. It then turned southward to "Keraka Devar Sandra," that is, the city of the son of (Li)sandros, ruler of the Jetherites; this is possibly Antioch, in the Dan region. From there the border passed the vicinity of Panias (mod. Banias), and continued past the Jewish Golan (Gaulanitis) to Kasfon (Kisfin, in the territory of Hippus), and along the borders of Batanea (Bashan) and Trachonitis (Zaroi–Sakka–Kenath–Nimrin to Sakkuta, i.e., Skeia, on the border of Hauran [Auranitis]). From this point the border continued southward along "the Great Desert Route," probably identical to the "new road" of Trajan. It passed close to Bostra (Bezer), Philadelphia (Rabbath-bene-ammon), Esbus (Heshbon), the Zered Brook, Taflith (et-Tafila), and went south to Gaia, in the vicinity of Petra and Rekem (identified with Petra). The border then continued along the "Heger" (Roman limes) to Raphia, and back up to Ascalon.

In this description of borders, despite the difficulty of identifying many of the names (particularly in the north, between the Mediterranean Sea and Panias), or even making an intelligent guess, it is clear that this boundary encompassed all Jewish settlement that existed immediately after the destruction of the Temple and before the easing of the halakhic rules for the land in various areas, by Rabbi Judah ha-Nasi (late second to early third centuries). He permitted this in the case of many cities, such as Sussita (Hippus), Beth-shean (Scythopolis), Panias, Kefar Zemah, and Beth Govrin (Eleutheropolis), and as a result, "the boundary of those returning from Babylonia" became only an abstract concept.

Stone relief of a menorah found at Naveh.

Aelia Capitolina 135 to 324 CE

When the Roman governor Tinneius Rufus "plowed up the Temple Mount," as the Talmud said, he was actually conducting a traditional Roman ceremony—that of founding a new city—whereby the founder or governor would plow a furrow (*pomerium*) along the site of the city's future walls. The city founded by Hadrian, upon the ruins of Jerusalem, was called "Aelia," after the emperor (Aelius Hadrianus), and "Capitolina," after the three Capitoline gods (Jupiter, Juno, Minerva).

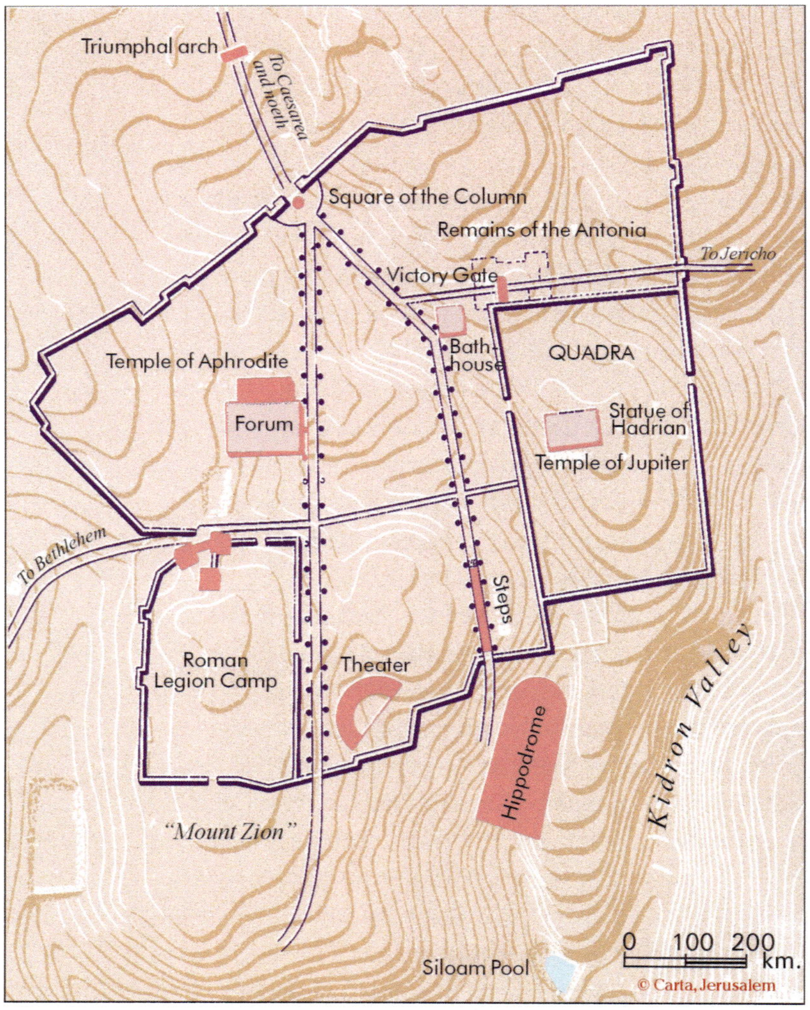

The city was typically planned on the model of a Roman army camp, square in shape with two streets intersecting at the center. In this case, however, for practical reasons, the plan deviated somewhat from the usual layout. A square with a column at its center was built near the northern gate. Branching off the square were the two colonnaded main streets. One led to the forum (marketplace), where a temple to Aphrodite stood nearby, and continued along the side of the Roman legionary camp that lay in the shadow of what remained of Herod's towers. The second street ran past the public bathhouses, where a side street led to the eastern gate. Above this side street a triumphal arch was built to mark the site of the Antonia fortress. On the Temple Mount platform (the "Quadra") stood the temple to Jupiter and in front of it, a statue of Hadrian on horseback. A second triumphal arch stood at the city's northern entrance. Here pilgrims would arrive from the coastal areas, from Caesarea or Joppa. To this day, this city plan can be recognized in the structure of Jerusalem's Old City.

Reconstructed southern section of the Cardo Maximus of Aelia Capitolina, Jerusalem (photo: Carole Raddato from Frankfurt, Germany)

RENEWAL OF JEWISH SETTLEMENT IN ERETZ ISRAEL:

The Wanderings of the Sanhedrin AFTER 70 CE

The Sanhedrin was exiled in ten stages.
Rosh Hashana 31b

After being exiled from Jerusalem, the Sanhedrin first resided in Jabneh. Following the religious persecutions by Hadrian, it moved to the Galilean town of Usha and, according to one theory, based on the Babylonian Talmud (*Rosh Hashana* 31b), returned temporarily to Jabneh, but was forced to return to Galilee.

The seat of the Sanhedrin then moved from Usha to Shepharam, and from there to Beth-shearim. R. Judah ha-Nasi ("the Prince"), during the last days of his presidency, transferred it to Sepphoris.

Finally, in the days of Judah ha-Nasi's grandson, R. Judah Nesiah, the Sanhedrin moved to Tiberias, where it remained until its dissolution.

However, even afterward its members continued to function in Tiberias under other names (e.g., *rashei ha-perek*, or academy lecturers), until Jerusalem again became the religious center after the Arab conquest.

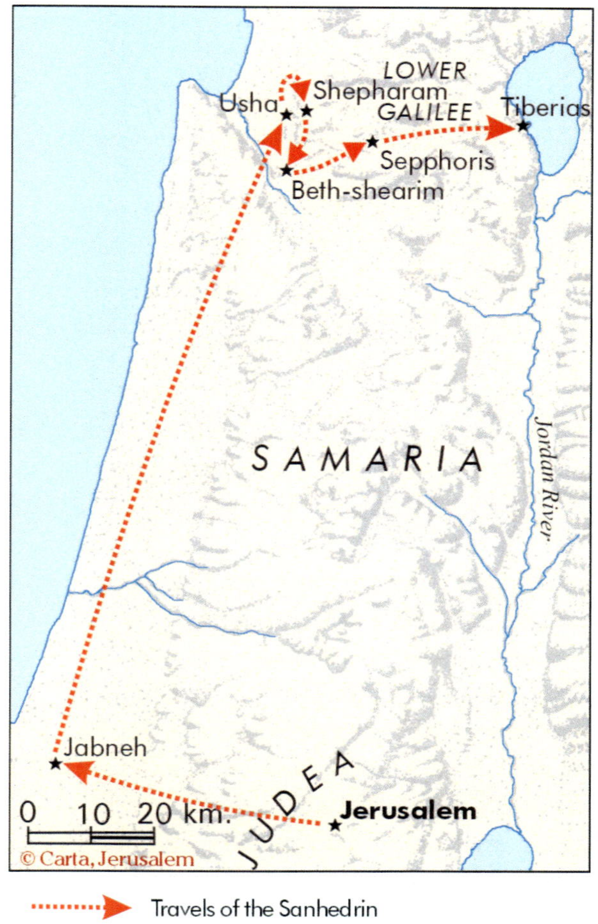

The Twenty-four Priestly Divisions

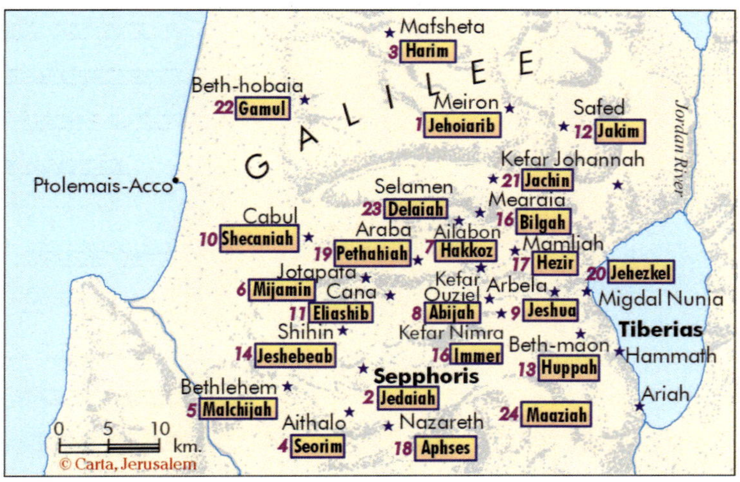

After the Bar Kokhba Revolt, twenty-four divisions (*mishmarot*) of priests (1 Chron. 24:7–18) who persisted in preserving their social unity, settled in various towns and villages in the Galilee. The list of these places, hinted at in the Jerusalem Talmud, was recorded in synagogue inscriptions and preserved in its entirety in *piyyutim* (liturgical poems). The nation apparently wished to memorize the order of the divisions—which also in a way served as a calendar—in anticipation of the resumption of their duties in the Temple, the rebuilding of which was expected at any time. Until the First Crusade, it was the custom in Palestinian synagogues, every Sabbath, to mention the priestly watch of the week, to recite the relevant *piyyut* and to offer a prayer for the priests to resume their duties.

משמרת ראשונה יהויריב מסרביי מרון
משמרת שניה ידעיה עמוק צפורים
משמרת שלישית חרים מפשטה
משמרת רביעית שערים עיתהלו
משמרת חמישית מלכיה בית לחם
משמרת ששית מימין יודפת
משמרת שביעית הקוץ עילבו
משמרת שמינית אביה כפר עוזיה
משמרת תשיעית ישוע ארבל
משמרת עשירית שכניה חבורת כבול
משמרת אחת עשרה אלישיב כהן קנה
משמרת שתים עשרה יקים פשחור צפת
משמרת שלוש עשרה חופה בית מעון
משמרת ארבע עשרה ישבאב חצפית שיחין
משמרת חמש עשרה בלגה מעריה יונית
משמרת שש עשרה אמר כפר נמרה
משמרת שבע עשרה חזיר ממליח
משמרת שמונה עשרה הפיצץ נצרת
משמרת תשע עשרה פתחיה אכלה ערב
משמרת עשרים יחזקאל מגדל נוניא
משמרת עשרים ואחת יכין כפר יוחנה
משמרת עשרים ושתים גמול בית חביה
משמרת עשרים ושלוש דליה צלמין
משמרת עשרים וארבע מעזיה חמת אריח

Fragments and reconstruction of inscription listing the 24 priestly courses, from mosaic floor of synagogue found at Caesarea.

The Jewish Settlement After 140 CE

Hadrian died three years after the fall of Bethther. His successor, Antoninus Pius, was a moderate man who adhered to Roman traditions. He did not leave Italy even once during his entire period of rule. Early in his reign, Palestine was still unruly, although the authorities slowly began to realize that it was not in their power to eradicate the Jews, and thus reconciled themselves to their presence. The emperor allowed the remaining sages to assemble in Usha, and reinstate the presidency of the Sanhedrin. Judaism once again became a "permitted religion," whereby the community was granted legal authorization and could hold property. Even the right to establish rabbinical courts in matters of finance (under the pretext of arbitration) was reinstated, as, with the weakening of Roman rule, was their right of criminal jurisdiction. The city councils of Tiberias and Sepphoris were also returned to Jewish hands. Although Jews were still forbidden to reside in Jerusalem, the authorities tended to "turn a blind eye" when they arrived in the city on pilgrimages, providing they stayed only a short time. The settlements in the south—in the Shephelah and the Jordan Valley—continued to exist, and the percentage of the urban Jewish population in these places increased. The Galilee remained almost entirely Jewish, with settlement based on the "householder" class, small farmers with "a field, a vineyard, and an olive grove." These farmers worked their fields themselves, without slave labor. The large estates of the wealthy and the families of various *nesi'im* (heads of the Sanhedrin), such as R. Tarfon, were outside the Galilee region: in the plain of Esdraelon, the Shephelah, or the Golan. Economically, the lot of the Jewish population improved in the generation following the religious persecutions by Hadrian. However, in the beginning, great damage was done, especially to the olive groves, and much of the land that was confiscated was passed on to foreign tax collectors. The economic crisis experienced by the Jewish community after the persecutions of Hadrian compelled the Jewish authorities to enact a number of emergency regulations, such as prohibiting the export of wheat, oil and wine—all essential products—and the raising of small livestock, i.e., goats and sheep, in afforested or cultivated areas. However, with their healthy economy, the Galilean Jews

overcame these difficulties, and the prohibitions were slowly lifted. Some Jews who had left the country returned, a few prisoners-of-war managed to return to their settlements, and those already settled never thought of leaving the Holy Land. This state of affairs made it easier for the Jewish leadership to reach a compromise with the Roman authorities by promising to keep the peace of the land.

The Jewish Diaspora in the Time of Antoninus Pius 138 TO 161 CE

Antoninus Pius; Hermitage Museum, St. Petersburg (photo: George Shuklin).

Peace within the Roman Empire remained undisturbed in the days of the "Antoninian" dynasty. This line of emperors, which came to the throne by way of adoption, ruled from the days of Nerva (96) to the death of Marcus Aurelius (180). Their reign was accompanied by economic growth, despite the troubling omens for the future.

The growth of the urban economy in the west of the empire led to the westward expansion of Diaspora Jewry in the second century. A few of the new communities formed as a result of external events, such as the expulsion of Jews from Rome to Sardinia under Tiberius, or the sale of Jews for slave labor after the Bar Kokhba Revolt.

However, the majority of Jews migrated voluntarily to commercial centers (mainly the provincial capitals) or to large military centers established along the empire's borders. The great majority of the

Jews of the Diaspora was still concentrated in the eastern part of the empire. Communities flourished especially in Asia Minor, as evidenced by the remains of splendid synagogues like the one at Sardis.

On the other hand, there was somewhat of a decline in Syrian Jewry, perhaps as a result of the discontent of non-Jews in the east to the revolts in the days of Trajan and Bar Kokhba. The situation of the Jewish communities in Greece is also known to have declined, but this was part of a general phenomenon: Greece at that time witnessed a decline in its population. The uprisings during Trajan's reign caused the near total destruction of the once large Egyptian Diaspora, as well as the eradication of Jewish communities in Cyrenaica and Cyprus; only in Alexandria did a small Jewish community remain.

Model of the Sardis synagogue at the Diaspora Museum, Israel.

In any event, the Jewish Diaspora was one of the reasons that the Roman government wished to make peace with the Jews of Palestine. The more so because some Jews lived beyond the borders of the empire, in Babylonia and other parts of the Parthian kingdom – in places beyond the reach of Roman rule.

In addition, the Jewish communities throughout the empire willingly accepted the leadership of the national authority reestablished in Palestine. With the exception of the *Fiscus Judaicus*, a poll tax of two *drachmae* levied on Jews from the time of Vespasian in place of the half-shekel tax for the Temple, the Jews of the Diaspora willingly continued to pay taxes to the *nesi'im* (pl. of *nasi*) of the Sanhedrin, and they received their emissaries with the highest esteem and followed their directives. The authorization given to these emissaries to teach and judge on behalf of the *nasi* (variously rendered as "prince," "patriarch," or "president") was recognized throughout the Diaspora and, when necessary, they were even authorized to suspend communal leaders.

The *nasi* and the Sanhedrin retained the exclusive right of consecrating the New Moon and intercalating the calendar by which Jewish festivals are determined. This proved to be an important tool for the unification of the Jewish people and the status of the *nasi* and the Sanhedrin throughout the Jewish Diaspora.

The Urbanization of the Land 63 to 330 CE

The Greek culture that predominated in the east, from the Hellenistic period onward, was clearly an urban one, and the cities became the main pillars of that culture from its inception. The Romans, heirs to the Hellenists in the east, continued the path of their predecessors, the kings of the Ptolemaic and Seleucid dynasties. Pompey "restored" the already-existing cities, especially on the northern and southern coasts of the country and in the northern part of Transjordan. Herod and his descendants, interested in creating an urban base for their regime, founded new cities or restored existing ones—Gentile (Sebaste, Caesarea Philippi [Panias]), mixed (Caesarea, Julias) and Jewish (Tiberias, Antipatris) alike.

The Jewish Revolt of 70 CE was a significant turning point in the urbanization of Palestine: a new city was founded (Neapolis), and several urban centers in Judea became independent cities (Joppa, Azotus, Jamnia, Sepphoris). The establishment of Provincia Arabia turned Charachmoba, Areopolis, Medeba and Esbus into cities. Hadrian's attempt to found Aelia Capitolina on the site of Jerusalem provoked the Bar Kokhba Revolt, but in the end he realized his original plan. After Hadrian, Septimius Severus in one year (200) founded Diospolis (formerly Lydda or Lod) and Eleutheropolis (Beth Govrin), and in this way caused the urbanization of two more areas. Heliogabalus (Nicopolis) and Diocletian (Maximianopolis, formerly Legio or Kefar-Othnay) completed the task of urbanization.

Almost the entire country was urbanized in this manner, apart from two kinds of areas: those with numerous Jews who opposed the Hellenistic culture and which, in the eyes of the Roman authorities, were not suited to an urban regime (these included the Upper Galilee and the Golan), and areas that included royal estates, which, because of their economic importance, the treasury wished to keep under its control. This was the fate of the lower Jordan Valley, on both its banks, and of three estates southeast of Gaza.

Overview of the ruins at Sepphoris (Diocaesarea) (photo: Carole Raddato from Frankfurt, Germany).

City Rivalries

The division of the land into city-centered entities raised the level of disputes and rivalries to that usually encountered by the competition of neighboring polities. This state of affairs endured throughout almost all of the third century when civil wars shook the Roman Empire. In the Midrash *Lamentations Rabbah* of the verse "The Lord hath commanded concerning Jacob, that his adversaries should be round about him" (Lam 1:17), lists neighboring cities which were rivals of each other. In this list, pairs of cities appear. Sometimes one is Jewish and the other Hellenistic or Samaritan, such as Tiberias–Hippus or Haifa–Castra (of the Samaritans), while other pairings consist of only two Jewish cities, or two Gentile cities, such as Lydda and Ono. The latter were within the boundaries of Lod but separated from the mother city in the late third century, following local skirmishes. Jericho with its mixed population and its rival, Jewish Naaran, were also mentioned in this list.

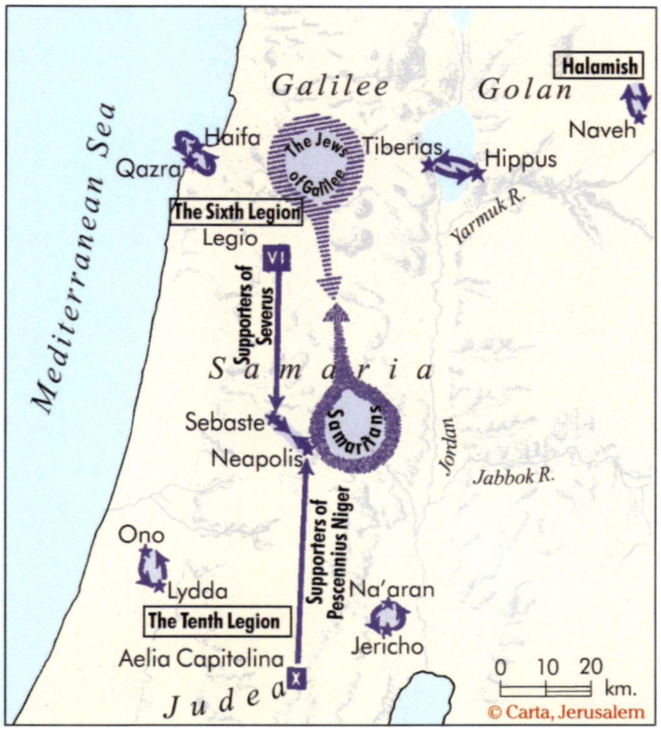

The struggles between the cities sometimes had far-reaching results. Thus, in 194 CE, a confrontation broke out between the Galilean Jews and the Samaritans whose center was in Neapolis. The Jews supported Septimius Verus in his struggle for the throne, and he was joined by the Sixth Legion. At the same time, the Samaritans and the Tenth Legion supported Pescennius Niger. Severus won, granting favors to his supporters while punishing his rivals and their cities.

Septimius Severus; from the excavations of Renier (1851) and Héron de Villefosse (1874) in Markouna, Algeria (now in the Louvre Museum, Paris).

(below) Denarius of Pescennius Niger (photo: Classical Numismatic Group, Inc. http://www.cngcoins.com).

General view of Nablus (Roman Neapolis) today (photo: Basel Quzeih).

The Third and Fourth Generations of *Tannaim* 115 to 175 CE

The mission of these generations of sages was to rehabilitate the nation following the religious persecutions of Hadrian, to establish a renewed national leadership, and to put together the Oral Law, a process which would culminate in the Mishnah, the monumental work of the next generation. Among the nation's outstanding leaders were the *aharonim* (latter elders), disciples of R. Akiva: R. Meir, who returned from Asya when the religious persecutions ended, and R. Simeon bar Yohai, who hid in a cave near Beqa' (Peki'in) with his son, R. Eleazar, and, as legend has it, lived there for thirteen years.

These sages first assembled in the Valley of Rimmon, together with several who had come up from Alexandria (e.g., R. Johanan ha-Sandlar). There was much camaraderie among the assembly: "If anyone did not have a prayer shawl, his friend would cut off half of his and give it to him." When they became aware of the change in the Roman authorities' relationship toward them, the sages gathered once again in Usha, where they reestablished the Sanhedrin. In time, Rabban Simeon ben Gamaliel was appointed *nasi*, R. Meir, *hakham* ("sage") and R. Nathan—who had emigrated from Babylonia—*av bet din* (head of the Sanhedrin). The call went out from Usha to the elders of Galilee: "Let everyone who is learned come and teach, and everyone who is not come and learn." Rabban Simeon slowly took control of the Sanhedrin. As a result, his opponents, led by R. Meir, left for Ardasqus and Tivon, near Usha. Many traditions are connected with R. Meir's later residency in Tiberias. R. Meir was also active in Beth-shean (Scythopolis) and also went south, to Lydda. In the end he was sent to intercalate the Hebrew calendar in Asya, where he died. R. Simeon bar Yohai was also separated from the court of the *nasi*. He purified Tiberias, stayed for some time in Tyre and Sidon, and died and was buried in Meiron. His son R. Eleazar died in Akhbarei, and with the help of the people of Birei was buried next to his father.

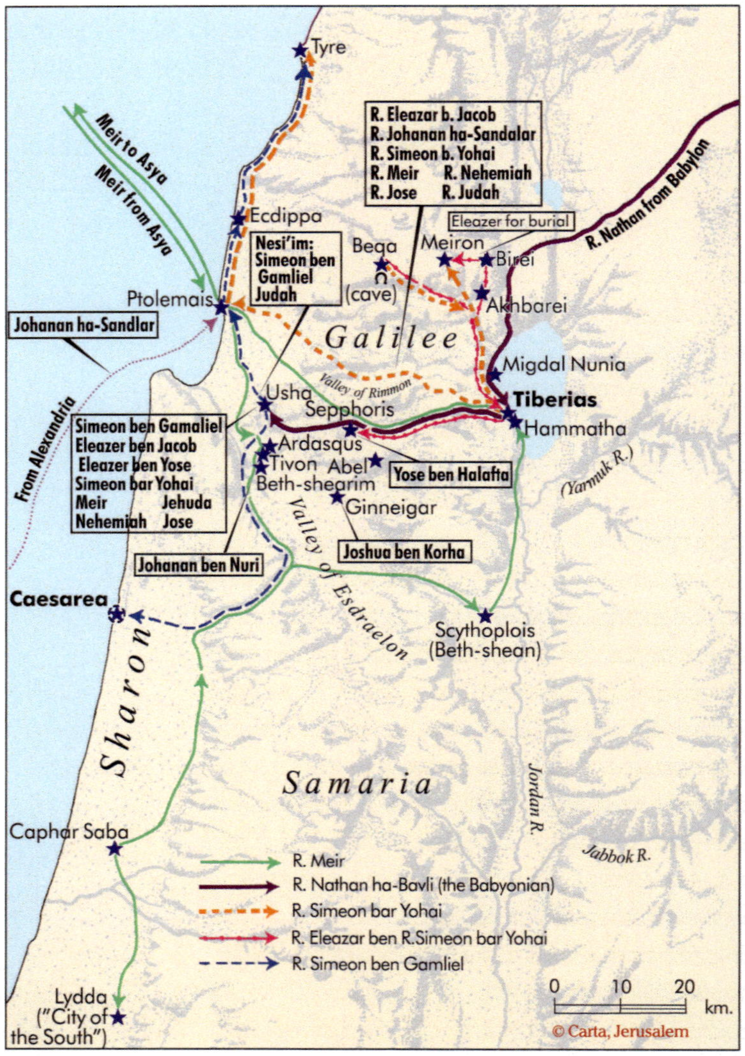

Rabban Simeon b. Gamaliel, together with Rabbi Yose and R. Judah, traveled to Ptolemais (Acco), Ecdippa (Achzib), and Caesarea, probably to make contact with the Roman procurator. Some traditions record his public activities in Sidon. Upon Simeon's death his eldest son, R. Judah, served as *nasi*, and during his time the presidency reached its zenith. It has been suggested that "the holy congregation of Jerusalem" mentioned in contemporary sources had lived in Jerusalem in the days of the Severan emperors, when the ban on Jewish settlement in the city was only lightly enforced.

Remains of the synagogue facade at Meiron (photo: Bukvoed).

Rabbi Judah ha-Nasi 135–220 CE

When Rabbi Akiva died, Rabbi was born
(*Kiddushin* 72b)

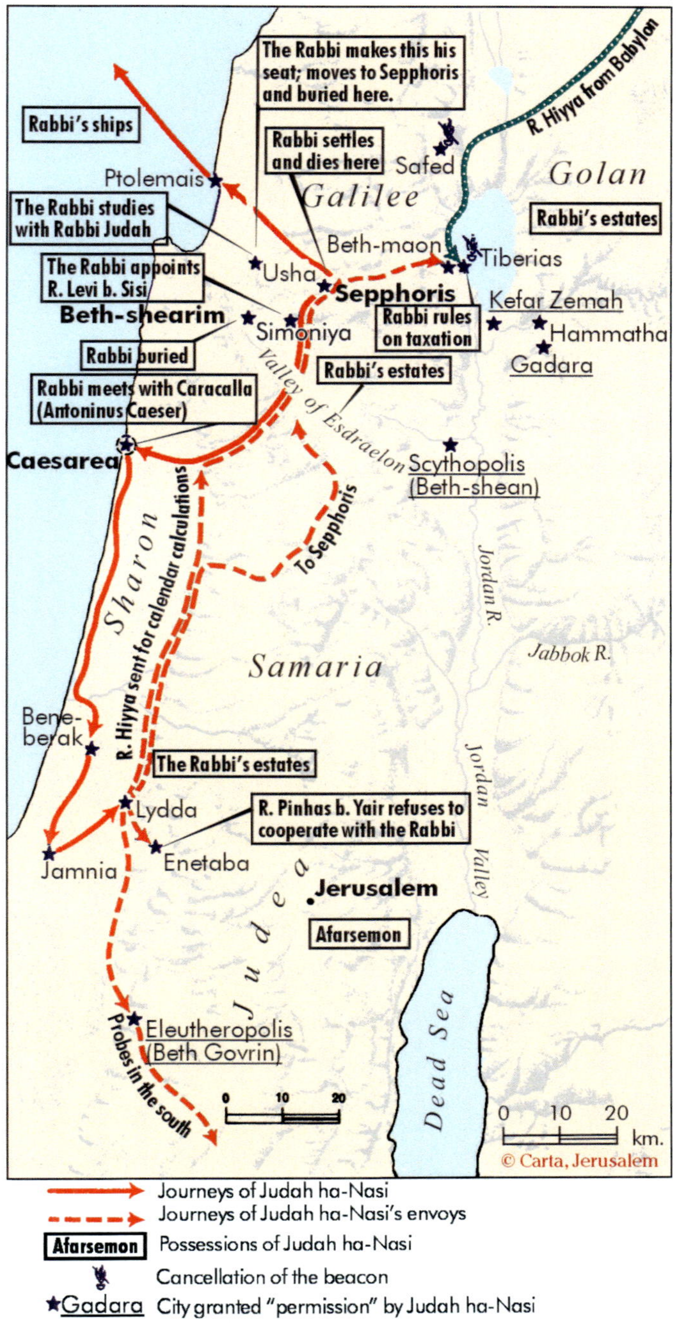

According to legend, Rabbi Judah ("Rabbi") was born in 135, on the same day that Rabbi Akiva died; he lived until 220. In his childhood he studied with Rabbis Eleazar ben Shammua, Simeon bar Yohai (in Tekoa), Judah ben Ilai (in Usha) and with other pupils of Rabbi Akiva. When he reached adulthood he settled in Beth-shearim, which he regarded as his city. In his final years, Rabbi transferred the presidency and the Sanhedrin to Sepphoris, where he died; he was buried, however, in Beth-shearim according to his last wishes.

Rabbi Judah exercised much authority. He completed and redacted the Mishnah. He enacted many rules, among them permission to exempt certain cities with a majority of foreign residents from observing the Sabbatical year (*shemittah*). He sent emissaries to Lod (Lydda) for intercalation of the year, and he sent R. Hiyya to Ein Tav to announce the new month (sanctification of the new moon). He himself visited Bene-berak, Lydda and Jabneh and he dispatched a committee of sages to the distant southern cities. He appointed teachers and judges in the provincial towns (such as Simoniya, where he sent R. Levi ben Sisi), and he sat in judgment on matters that concerned the large cities, e.g., the matter of taxes in Tiberias. The estates he owned in the Golan, the Jezreel Valley, the vicinity of Lod, and in the Jordan Valley yielded goods which were sent abroad in ships he owned. This allowed Rabbi to hold a luxurious court with golden vessels, mules, as well as servants who spoke fine Hebrew.

His relations with the Roman authorities were very good. His friend "Antoninus" (probably Caracalla, son of Severus, who ruled from 211 to 217) bestowed on him estates and also met him in Caesarea. Most of the sages were obedient to Rabbi. Only Rabbi Pinhas ben Yair the Pious, who lived in the south, remained aloof and refused to cooperate with him. The memory of Rabbi Judah ha-Nasi's greatness remained alive for generations: "Since the days of Moses and until Rabbi, we have not found Torah and greatness in one place."

The cave of Rabbi Judah ha-Nasi at Beth-shearim (photo:Cesar Yeudkin).

Migration Routes from Babylonia to Eretz Israel

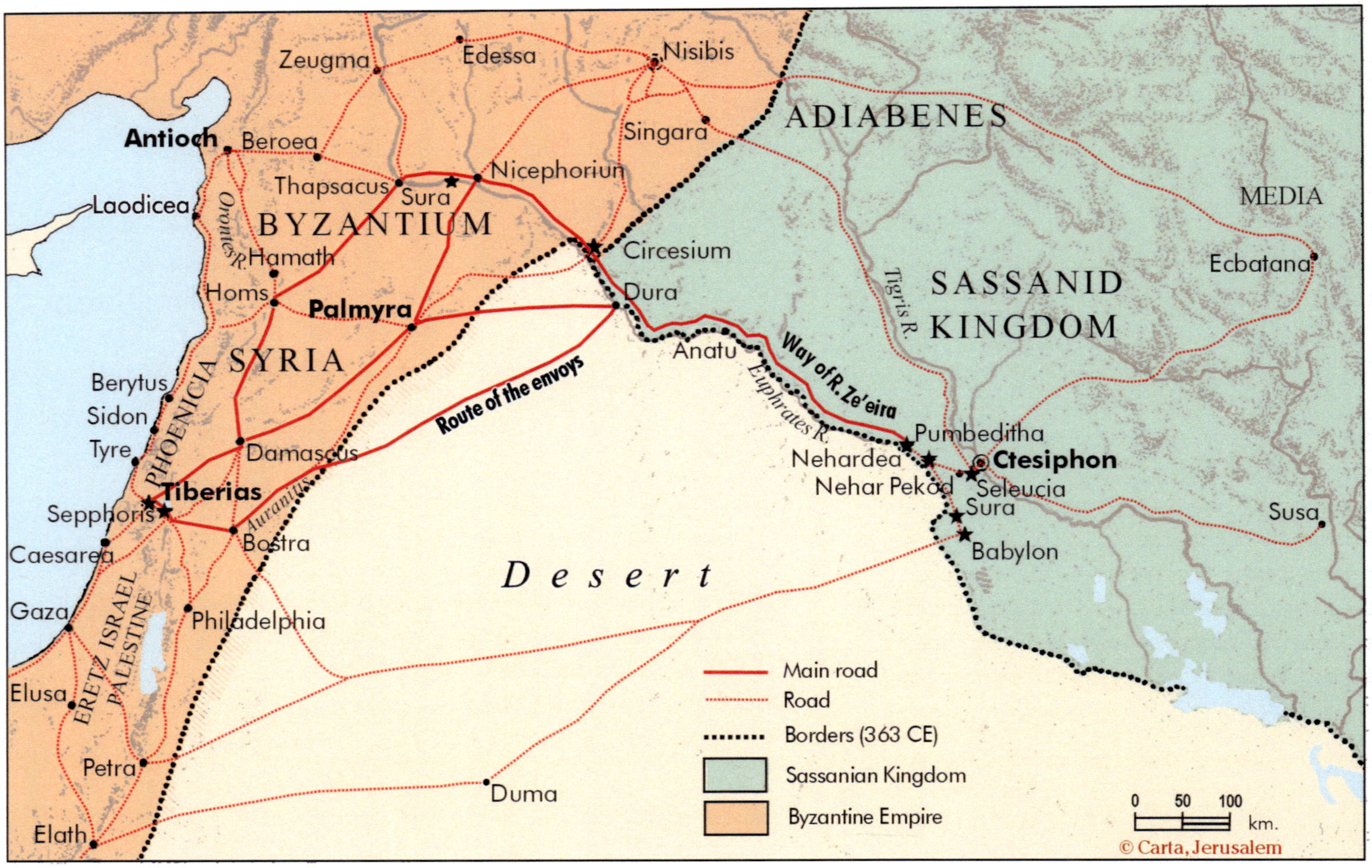

The ties between the Babylonian Diaspora and the land of the Patriarchs, which had already existed in the days of the Return to Zion, were never broken as long as there remained a strong Jewish presence in the Land. The route generally used was that which ran along the Euphrates River; it was chosen by R. Ze'eira who, despite the ban imposed on him by his teacher, Rav Judah, decided to go and study Torah with R. Johanan himself. Starting out from Dura the travelers went to Circesium, passed Sura (in Syria, not to be confused with Sura in Babylonia), and at Thapsacus (Tiphsah) they turned south to Homs, finally reaching Damascus. Another possible route was the direct one from Dura to Palmyra (Tadmor; or from Circesium to Palmyra), and from there straight to Damascus via Auranitis (the Hauran). The Adiabenes and Medes moved westward on the route taken by the patriarch Abraham—along the Tigris River and then in the land of Haran (Nisibis–Edessa), up to the bridge over the Euphrates at Zeugma, and from there via Beroea (Aleppo) and Antioch.

A particularly short route was "The Way of the Emissaries," which took only seven days (unlike the two weeks required by a more conventional route). Emissaries on behalf of the Sanhedrin traveled directly through the desert to bring the Babylonian Jews news of the intercalation of the calendar and the consecration of the New Moon as determined by the sages of Eretz Israel. Other routes passed through the very heart of the desert—from Petra to Babylon or from Elath via Duma—but these were used chiefly by caravans of Nabateans and their successors, the Saracens.

The monumental arch and remains at Palmyra (photo: Bernard Gagnon).

ERETZ ISRAEL IN THE DAYS OF THE AMORAIM

The First Generation of *Amoraim* 225 TO 260 CE

On his deathbed Rabbi Judah ha-Nasi gave these instructions: "My son Simeon [is to be] *hakham* (sage), my son Gamaliel *nasi* (patriarch), Hanina bar Hama shall preside" (*Ketubbot* 103b). The group was largely deprived of its leadership after the Rabbi's death. The deciding power in the nation's affairs passed to the heads of the Sanhedrin and a distinction began to be made between the patriarchy and the Sanhedrin.

After the passing of Rabbi Judah ha-Nasi, R. Aphes ha-Dromi became *av bet din* (head of the Sanhedrin) in Sepphoris, followed by R. Hanina bar Hama, a disciple of Judah ha-Nasi. The *batei hamidrash* (lit., "houses of study") were somewhat dispersed: R. Hoshaya founded an academy at Caesarea, and R. Joshua b. Levi became one of the leading sages at Lydda. In the period of the *amoraim* news surfaced about the sages of Naveh in Transjordan: the "*rabbanan di-Naveh*." Still, the sages from the various places were accustomed to assembling in Sepphoris and in Hammatha (Hammath Gader) during the bathing season there, as well as during public missions, such as those of R. Joshua b. Levi and R. Hanina bar Hama to the Roman governor at Caesarea. When R. Joshua returned from a mission to Rome, R. Hanina went to Ptolemais to welcome him.

During this period, Caracalla ("Antoninus Caesar"), son of Septimius Severus, was murdered, causing a political crisis in the Roman Empire. In the beginning the reigning emperors were of Syrian origin, such as Heliogabalus (218–222) and Alexander Severus (222–235), who were benevolent toward the Jews. They were followed by a period of chaos, power changes, and incessant wars between the various claimants to the throne. Each of these pretenders recruited an army, levied taxes, and commandeered supplies for his soldiers, thereby impoverishing the citizenry. The first indication of distress was the permission to work the land during the Sabbatical year granted by R. Yannai, who resided with his *beth midrash* in Akhbarei. More than others, he and his pupils, who engaged in agricultural work, felt the heavy burden of the property tax. The political crisis brought with it a sapping of Roman power and the easing of old bans, such as that on Jews entering Jerusalem. Thus R. Hanina bar Hama and R. Joshua b. Levi went up to the Holy City. At this time, too, with the weakening of the regime, a feeling of greater security spread among the Jews, who began to lay the groundwork for a change in the ambivalent relationship with Rome.

This generation also began the compilation and editing of Oral Law literature not included in the Mishnah. The Tosefta—the complement and extension to the Mishnah—was arranged, as were halakhic *midrashim* (homiletic interpretations). First steps were also made in the adaptation to the Mishnah of interpretations and customs—the core of the Palestinian ("Jerusalem") Talmud.

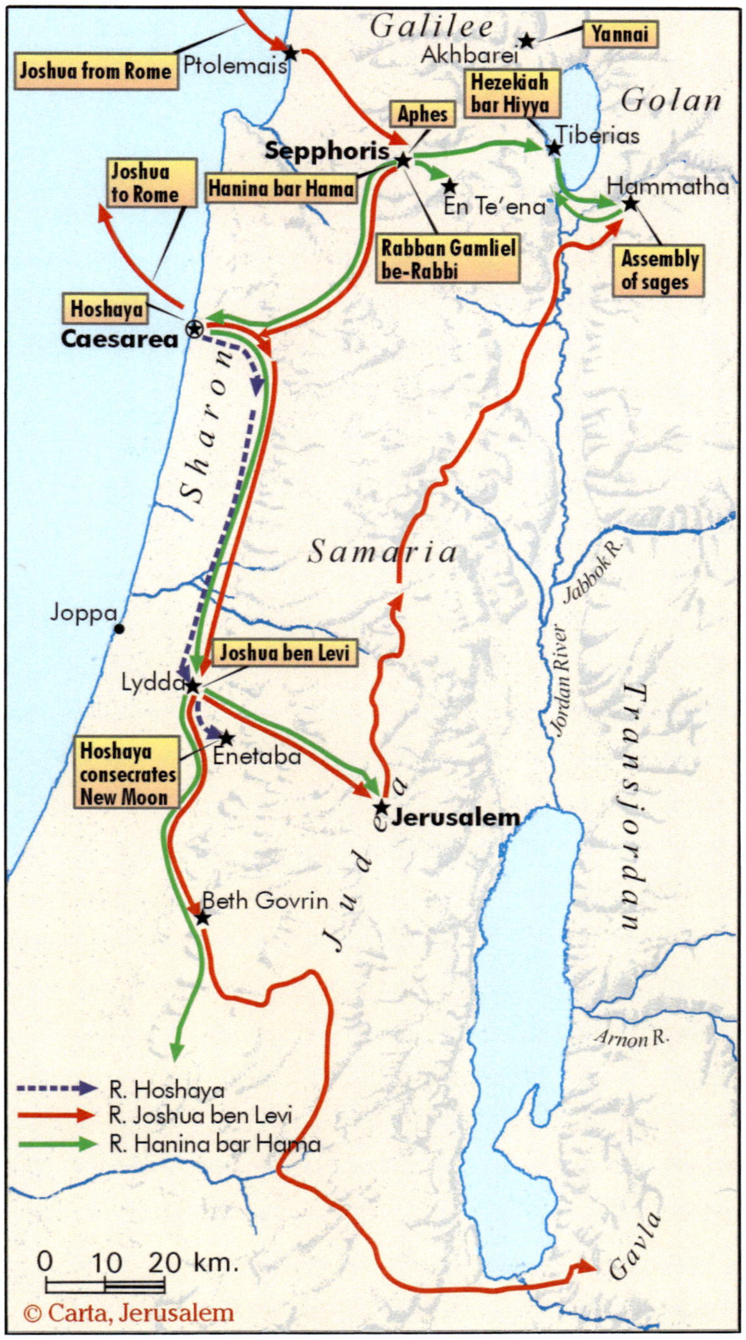

Area overlooking Hammath Gader, looking east (photo S. Magal).

Tiberias

The Sanhedrin went into exile from Sepphoris to Tiberias…and from there they will be redeemed.
Rosh Hashanah 31b

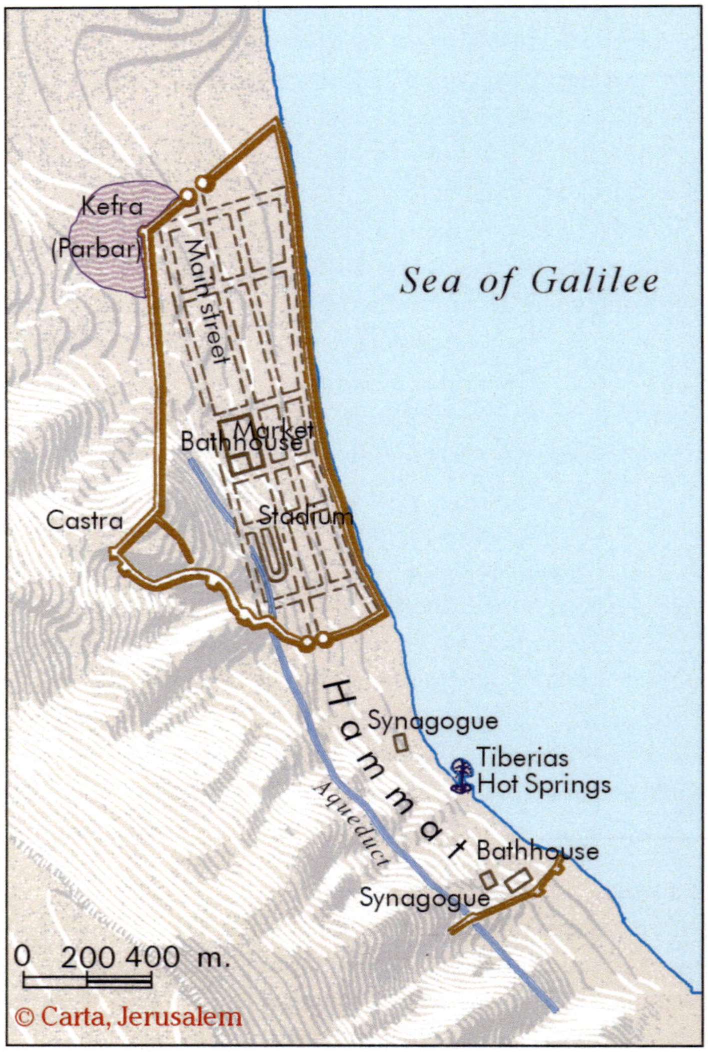

The city of Tiberias was founded between 18 and 20 CE by Herod's son, Herod Antipas, on the remains of biblical Rakkath. For a long time it was regarded by the sages as unclean, because of its mixed population of freed slaves, and foreigners, and because Antipas settled here. Another reason seems to have been the discovery of the many graves that were discovered within its boundaries at the time of its construction. Ben Azzai and mainly R. Simeon bar Yohai purified the city. During the second generation of *amoraim*, Tiberias became the seat of the Sanhedrin and later of the *nasi* (president). It was the administrative center of the Jews in the Land of Israel and the spiritual center for the Diaspora as a whole. It remained as such even after the termination of the presidency in the early fifth century. After the Arab conquest of Jerusalem, the Yeshiva, which had succeeded the Sanhedrin, returned to Tiberias, the Holy City.

Talmudic sources provide much information about the structure of Tiberias, which stretched between the suburb of Kefara, on the one side, and nearby Hammath, with its famous hot springs, on the other. From the sources we learn about the city's fortress (Castra), stadium, markets (such as the woodcutters' market), *batei midrash* and synagogues of the various communities, such as those of the *Tarsiim* (i.e., the linen-workers) and of the Babylonians, the *boule* (municipal council), and the public bathhouses. The talmudic sources also mention the economic life of the city, which included various workshops, such as for glass, mats, sacks, and hides. Wheat, figs, and grapes were cultivated in the area. There were also many fishermen and fishponds for cultivating fish. Its famed hot springs attracted many visitors.

The archaeological finds show that in the Roman period the city was to the south of present-day Tiberias, and to the north of Hammath. Roman Tiberias was surrounded by a wall, built in the time of R. Judah II Nesiah. Its gates were flanked by round towers. The main street (Cardo) ran from north to south with markets and baths nearby and perhaps also the stadium. The city wall extended to the top of the hill where Antipas's palace (the Castra) stood. The city's aqueduct ran from Nahal Yavne'el in the south with extensions to Beth Yerah and Hammath. Remains of two synagogues, a bathhouse and a wall have been uncovered in Hammath.

Modern Tiberias as viewed from the gravesite of Rabbi Meir, looking north (photo: Tiberias municipality).

Sanctification of the New Moon and Intercalation of the Year

One of the most important tools for the tightening of the connections between the Diaspora and Eretz Israel and the strengthening of the central national authority (the *nasi* and the Sanhedrin) was that of setting the beginning of the month and intercalating the year (by adding the month of second Adar); this was the exclusive right of the sages of Eretz Israel who thereby also determined the date of the festivals. The custom of regulating the feast days according to observations of the nature and testimonies of witnesses who saw the new moon without resorting to astronomical calculations, continued after the destruction of the Temple. The astronomical calculations, while known and consulted, were kept secret.

After the destruction of Jerusalem, the sanctification of the new moon and the intercalation of the year were determined in Jabneh. However, following the decrees of Hadrian and the uprooting of the Jewish population from Judea, the question arose if these actions could be performed in Galilee. In the early years following the restoration of the Sanhedrin in Galilee, these actions were indeed performed there (first in the Rimmon Valley and later in Usha) according to the rule: "The intercalation of the year is performed nowhere but in Judea, but if it has been intercalated in Galilee—it is intercalated." However, as relations between the *nesi'im* and Rome improved, these functions were once again performed in Lydda (Lod), the main city of Judea.

During the armed conflict between the supporters of Niger and those of Severus, emissaries who had been dispatched by Rabbi Judah ha-Nasi to facilitate the intercalation of the year were attacked. After that incident intercalation was performed in Galilee. Due to the objection of the sages in the south, however, the sanctification of the moon remained in Judea and sages from the centers of the Sanhedrin traveled to Judea, returning north after having completed their task. Conceivably, the sanctification of the new moon in Judea lasted until the time of Hillel II, in the fourth century, when the methods of calculating the Jewish calendar became public knowledge.

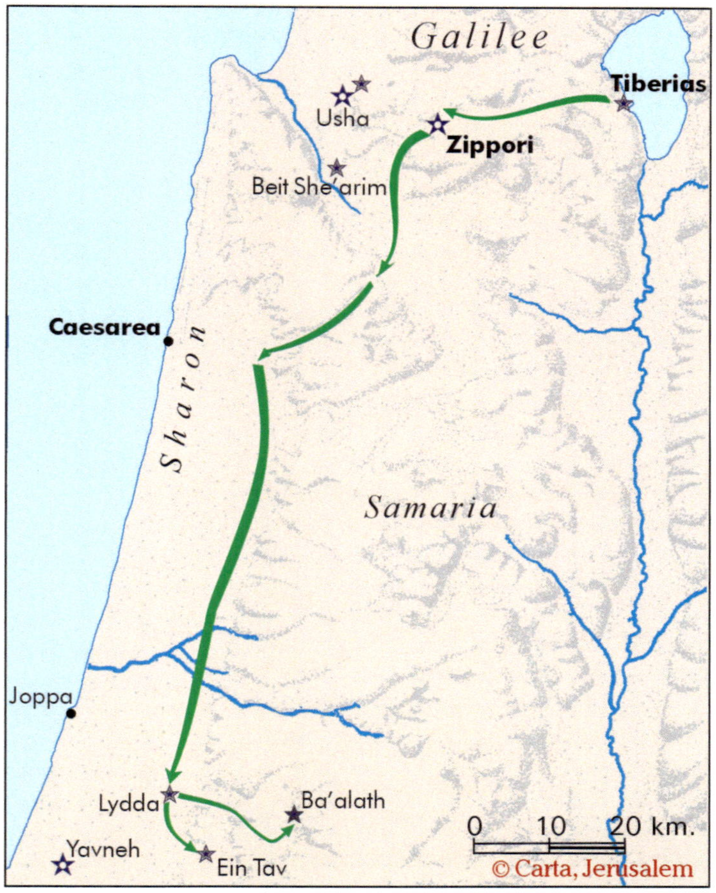

☆ Place where the Sanhedrin sat for the ritual blessing of the new moon and the leap year

★ Other places where the Sanhedrin sat

The Second Generation of *Amoraim* 260 TO 290 CE

Standing at the head of this generation were the sages R. Johanan, its central figure, and his disciple R. Simeon b. Lakish (known by his Hebrew acronym, "Resh Lakish"). Both resided in Tiberias.

Mosaic floor of synagogue at Hammath Tiberias (photo: A. Alon).

R. Johanan would visit his teacher, R. Hoshaya, in Caesarea, and travel to Gennesar and Mamliah, and perhaps also to Naveh. Resh Lakish was active in both Hukkok and Gennesar; he often stayed in Bostra and even went outside the Holy Land. When R. Johanan reached his golden years, R. Eleazar b. Pedat became *av bet din* at Tiberias. Both passed away the same year (279). R. Yose bar Hanina, who had ties with the sages of the south, resided in Caesarea. R. Simeon b. Pazzi, R. Simlai, and R. Samuel b. Nahman were active in Lydda.

The ongoing halakhic deliberations at this time served as the basis for the Jerusalem Talmud. Ties with Babylonia were strengthened, and many disciples came to Tiberias while a few, like R. Eleazar b. Pedat, even settled in the land. Furthermore, numerous emissaries were sent to Babylonia to pass on the teachings of the Palestinian sages. In the days of R. Johanan, the crisis in the Roman Empire reached its peak. The emperor Valerian fell prisoner to the Persians (260), and the Palmyrene rulers, Zenobia and Vaballathus her son, seized the eastern half of the empire. Although there were

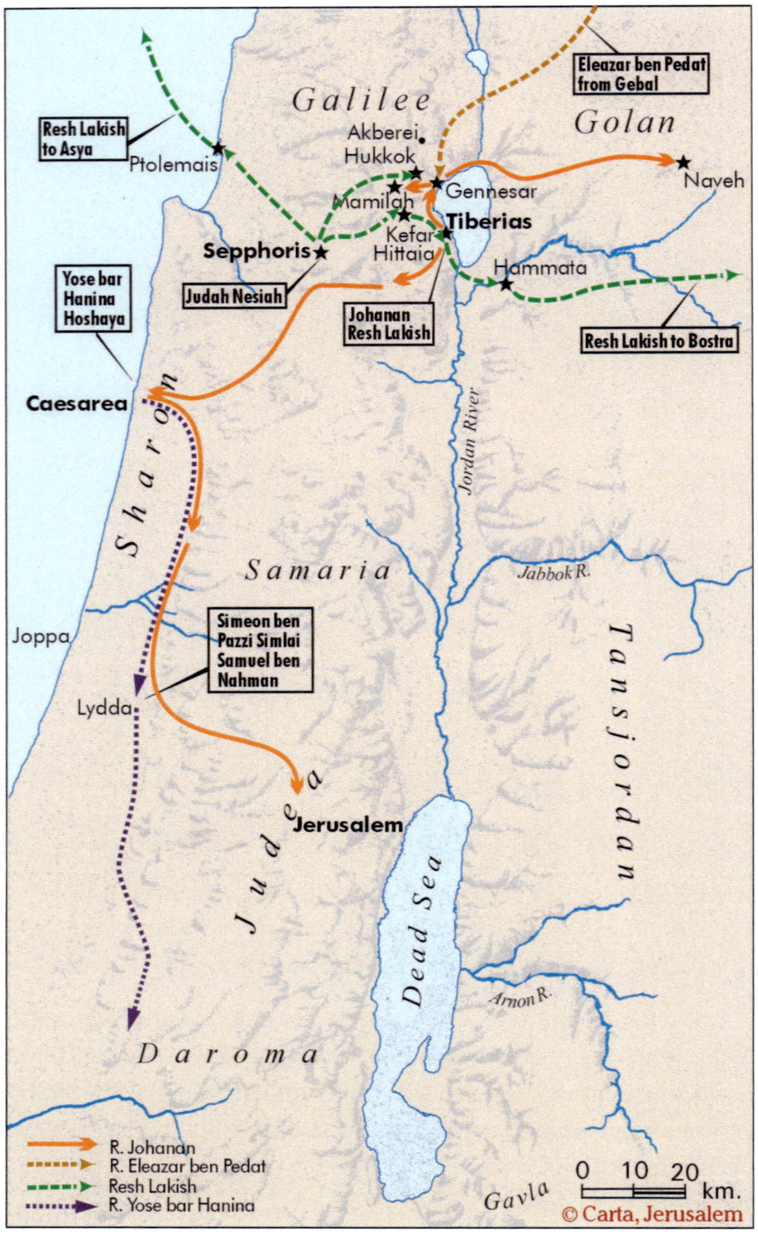

And it was said that Rabbi Johanan ruled in Eretz Israel for eighty years.
Letter of Rav Sharira Gaon

contacts with the court of Palmyra (visited by R. Ammi, one of the younger scholars of this generation), the sages remained wary of the regime. In 271 the emperor Aurelian captured Palmyra and restored Roman rule to the entire east, including Palestine.

In the same period, the economic fallout from the political crisis was severe: taxes multiplied; money lost in value; famine and plagues were prevalent. The economic distress weakened the status of the *nasi* (Rabbi Judah Nesiah), and caused much friction between the sages and the *nasi*. Resh Lakish would speak harshly in front of the *nasi*, and once was forced to flee Tiberias and hide in Kefar Hittaia. In the end, the rights of the *nasi* were restricted, and many of his functions, both theoretical and practical, were assumed by the sages. The economic crisis largely undermined the status of Palestinian Jewry in relation to Babylonian Jewry and revived messianic hopes among the people. It also appears that in this generation the percentage of Jews in the Galilee and in all of Palestine fell dramatically. On the other hand, access to Jerusalem was almost unrestricted, so that R. Johanan could say: "Let all those who want to go up [to Jerusalem] go up!" (*Baba Batra* 65b).

The Administrative Reforms of Diocletian 284 TO 305 CE

"The strong man" who put an end to the crisis in the Roman Empire was the emperor Diocletian, who ruled from 284 to 305. He made a number of changes in order to strengthen central rule, to ensure stability and to streamline the administration and the army. He divided the Empire into four large units: the West (Britain, France and Spain); Italy and its provinces in the Alps and in Africa; Illyricum (the Balkan peninsula); and the East, which included the Land of Israel. Each unit had its own administrative and financial organization. Two units were headed by Caesars of higher rank (the "Augusti") while the other two were headed by Caesars of lower rank who could replace the higher ones when necessary.

In order to create a mobile military reserve unit Diocletian divided the Roman army into two: the superior half was stationed in the royal courts while the other half was stationed along the borders. The soldiers of the latter (*limitanei*) were allowed to receive tracts of land for cultivation. At the same time, Diocletian separated the military command from the civil administration.

This arrangement restricted the governors' potential to rebel against the emperor. To this end Diocletian made further efforts by subdividing the large provinces. He also tried to curb inflation by putting a limit on prices for many commodities and services. He also tried to stabilize the coin of realm; but his attempts in finance were not as successful as those he made in the political and military spheres.

Head of Diocletian; Istanbul Archaeological Museum (photo: Giovanni Dall'Orto).

In the Land of Israel (the emperor stayed in Tiberias in 286) Diocletian initiated various reforms, such as the transfer of the Tenth Legion to Aila together with that of the

Remains of the agora *(marketplace) at Tyre (photo: Heretiq).*

command of a *dux Palaestinae* that seems to have extended to the Zered Brook. Many infantry and cavalry units, including archers and camel riders, were stationed along the main roads, mainly the *Limes* line, opposite the Arabian desert. Others were stationed between Maon and the Dead Sea, to prevent the invasion of nomads from the Sinai desert. Another territory, *dux Arabiae*, with two legions, was responsible for the region between the Zered Brook and the border of Trachonitis. One legion (the Cyrenean Third Legion) remained in Bostra, while the second (the Fourth Legion named after Mars) was stationed in Legio, east of Rabbath Moab.

Certain reforms were also made in the civil administration: Dora, the Negeb and all of Transjordan south of the Arnon River were handed over to the ruling authority of *Syria Palaestina*. As compensation, the governor of Arabia received Batanea and Auranitis. Within Palestine steps were taken to complete the process of urbanization, such as founding the city of Diocletianupolis (Sarafia) near Ascalon, and two cities named after Diocletian's co-emperor, Maximian, one in Legio (Kefar Othnai), and the other in Saccaea in Auranitis.

Diocletian also made the tax burden more equitable by creating the cadaster (land registration) system. The village lands were measured anew and their boundaries were marked. A large number of such boundary stones testifying to these actions was discovered in the regions of the Golan and the Bashan. The road network too was improved and additional fortifications were built along the *Limes*.

When Diocletian the king came here he ordered: "All nations will offer libation except for the Jews."
(JT *Avodah Zarah* 5:44d)

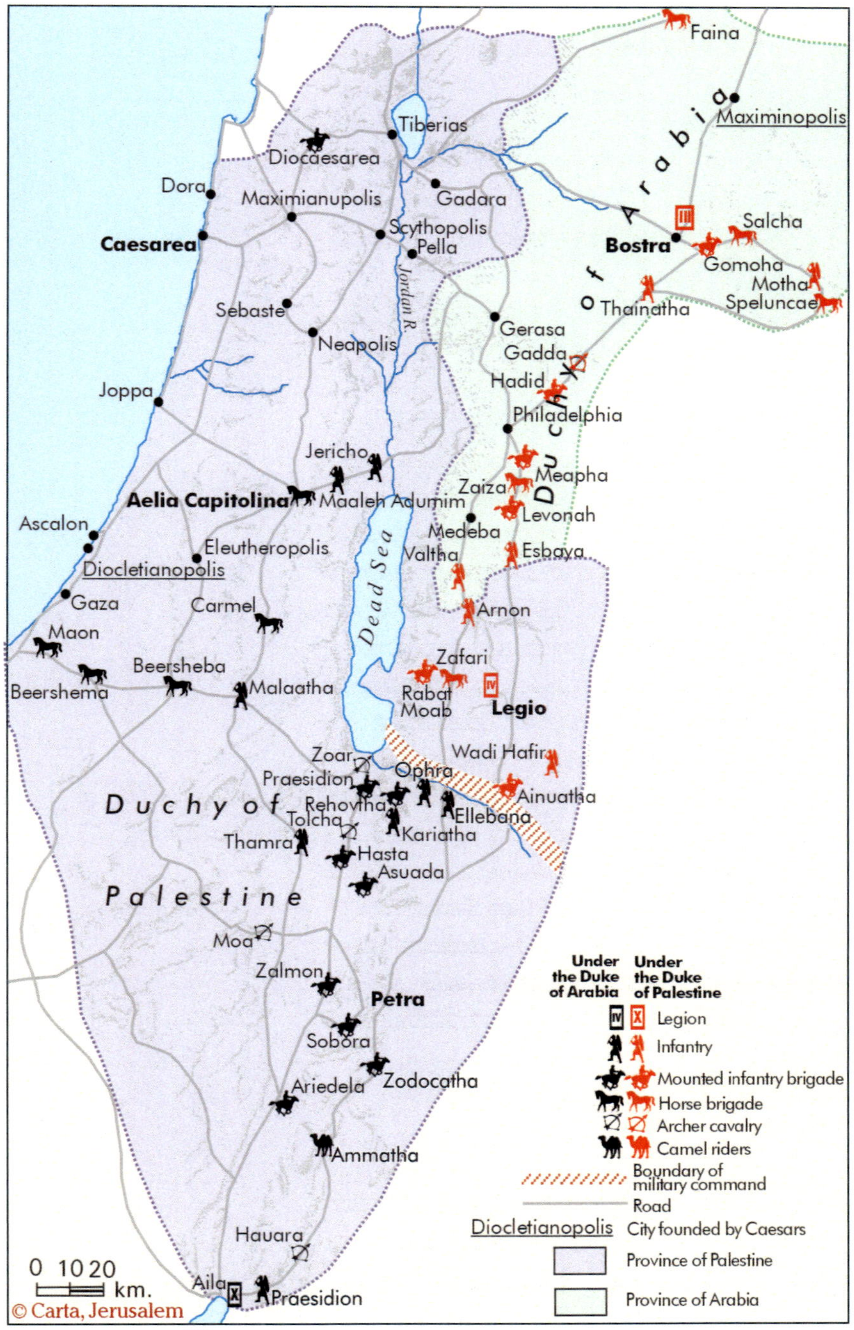

Concerning religious matters, Diocletian persecuted the Christians, whom he regarded as dangerous to the Empire. His attitude toward the Jews was quite positive. During his stay in Tiberias, he met with the *nasi* and exempted the Jews from having to bring sacrifices to the gods, a burden imposed on the rest of the empire's citizens. The talmudic sources tell of many works done by his decree, such as the building of a dam on the Hams Sea in Syria and the renewal of the market in Tyre, to name a few. During Diocletian's visit to Tyre "Rabbi Hiyya son of Abba was seen to pass over tombs in Tyre in order to see him," despite Rabbi Hiyya being a priest (and thus forbidden to enter cemeteries). This attests to the strong impression the personality of Diocletian made on the sages, even though it was told of him that in his youth "he herded pigs in Tiberias."

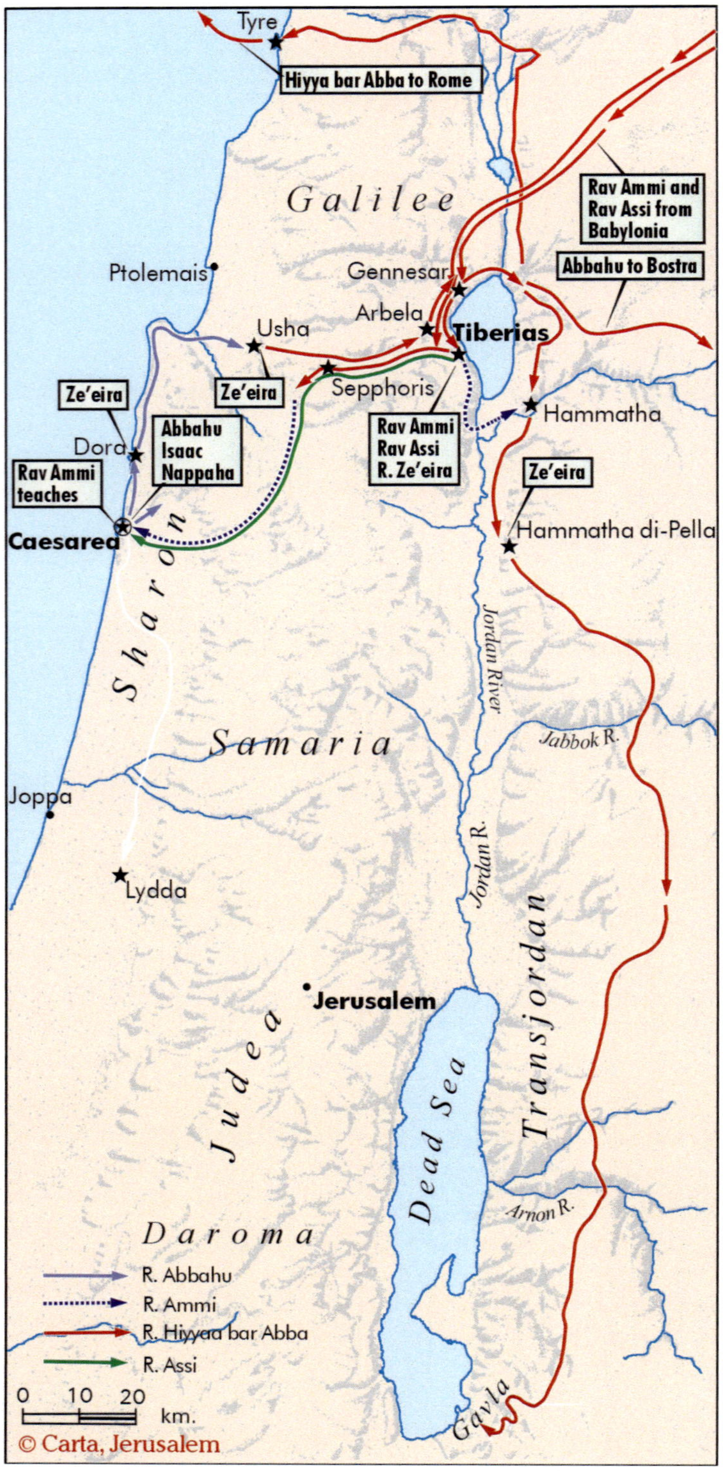

The Third Generation of *Amoraim* 280 TO 320 CE

The third generation of *amoraim* saw a major turning point in the history of the ancient world: Emperor Diocletian and his heirs solved the political and economic crisis, and from the days of Constantine onward, the Christian "heresy" became the state religion. This radical change disturbed many of the generation, and some, such as the Comes Joseph, abandoned the religion of their forefathers.

The Jewish nation was headed by the *nasi* who, despite his diminished status, was still respected along with the Sanhedrin, headed by R. Ammi and R. Assi, in Tiberias. Meanwhile, though, the academy at Caesarea had become more prestigious and with it the status of R. Abbahu, its head. This sage also had close contacts with the authorities and he often visited Tiberias. R. Judah bar Simon was active in this generation in Lydda. Notably, all the generation's leaders, apart from R. Abbahu, were of Babylonian origin.

The rise of Christianity caused the renewal of disputes with the "heretics" (Judeo-Christians). R. Abbahu was among the defenders of the faith. However, despite internal and external hardships, the creation and compilation of material for the Jerusalem Talmud continued unabated.

The Spread of Christianity in Eretz Israel; The Comes Joseph 70 TO 360

Although Christianity evolved among the Jews in the Land of Israel where Jesus and his first disciples were active, the new religion did not take root in the land of Jesus' birth, except in the Gentile areas. The activity of the first disciples resulted in the establishment of a Judeo-Christian community in Jerusalem, which survived until the Bar Kokhba revolt. Christian communities may also have existed in Lydda and Jaffa as early as the first century. In Caesarea and Acco, Christianity spread mainly among the foreign residents. Christian communities may have existed also in Capernaum and other Galilean villages, as well as in Pella, where Christians from Jerusalem settled before the city's siege by Titus. In the second century, Christian communities populated a number of major cities in the Land of Israel, such as Ashdod, Neapolis, Bostra and Philadelphia (Rabbath-ammon). A Jewish-Christian settlement existed in Kokhaba in the Golan.

The spread of Christianity increased at a faster rate in the third century. At that time the disciples' activities reached their peak. The apostles took advantage of the general deterioration of the traditional Greco-Roman religion, which at the time lost its appeal throughout the ancient world. Sharp conflicts arose between the Jews in the Diaspora and the Christians. During the third century, too, Christian communities were established in most of the cities

To receive permission, by order of the Emperor, to build Messianic churches in the Jewish towns and villages.
The acts of Joseph according to Epiphanius

in the Land of Israel, except for the purely Jewish cities in the Galilee—e.g., Sepphoris and Tiberias.

Christianity came into its own after Emperor Constantine defeated his rival Lycian, at which time the turmoil following the resignation of Diocletian and Maximian in 305 came to an end. Constantine himself did not convert to Christianity until late in life, but supported it in various ways. In 312 he declared in Milan that Christianity from now on would be a recognized religion, thus allowing open organization of churches everywhere. After his victory over Lycian (324), Constantine called a general synod in Nicaea, subsequently called the First Ecumenical Council of Nicaea. Only fourteen bishops from the Land of Israel, headed by Eusebius of Caesarea, participated. His colleague from Jerusalem, Macarius, persuaded the emperor and his mother Helena the Pious to build three churches, two in Jerusalem and one in Bethlehem, commemorating the birth of Jesus, his burial and his ascension to heaven. Because of Constantine's favorable attitude toward Christianity, many communities emerged in various towns and villages throughout the Land of Israel. Cities such as Gaza and Ascalon, whose main population remained faithful to Hellenism, had to fight for their religious identity.

The Jews too became aware of new dangers to their lives. Even though Constantine's legislation did little harm to their standing, Christian leaders whom he inspired did much to restrict the independence of the Jews. Thus, Constantine encouraged a converted Jew by the name of Joseph, who had once been one of the heads of the president's court. He endowed him with the title "Comes" (the emperor's companion), and supported his intentions to build churches in some of the Galilean Jewish centers in which Christians had yet no foothold (such as Sepphoris and Tiberias), or in places holy to Christians (such as Capernaum and Nazareth). Joseph's activity was not always successful. For example, he did not succeed in his attempt to convert a building in Tiberias into a Christian church that was originally intended for Hadrian but not completed because of Jewish opposition. Christian bishops from Tiberias and Sepphoris did attend church councils in the fifth century, but these cities remained almost totally Jewish. Joseph died excommunicated and lonely in Beth-shean, the provincial capital. Christianity in general had little influence on Jewish society and the Jewish-Christian communities grew smaller in the fourth century, and became assimilated in the Christian world at large.

In the fourth century, Christianity began to penetrate many of the villages in Eretz Israel and in the fifth century Christians became the majority of the population. This situation changed only after the break between the Orthodox church and the Monophysites (mainly of Syria and Egypt) following the Council of Chalcedon (451).

Restored Roman-Byzantine remains at Caesarea (photo: Grand Parc—Bordeaux, France).

The Fourth Generation of *Amoraim* 320 to 360

During the fourth generation (320–360) Eretz Israel passed into the hands of a Christian emperor (324), and the authorities put increasing pressure on the Jews—political, religious, and economic. The heads of the Tiberias academy at this time were R. Jeremiah, of Babylonian origin, and after him R. Jonah and R. Yose. R. Jeremiah also saw to it that the burdensome taxes imposed on the city's inhabitants were evenly distributed. He often went on public business to cities such as Ptolemais, Gaulan, Sogane and Lavi, and went to the Dead Sea area (Zoar?). R. Jonah resided for a while in Tyre. R. Yose lived to a ripe old age, and visited Dora and Eshtemoa. R. Haggai, also of Babylonian origin, joined the rabbis in Tiberias. R. Aha was active and taught at Lydda; both R. Jonah and R. Yose came to pay homage, and he in turn would go to Tiberias. R. Aha also served as a teacher in Emmaus and an inspector in Arabiya. In Caesarea, outstanding among his generation, was R. Isaac b. Eleazar, who also dealt with the halakhic laws of sea travel.

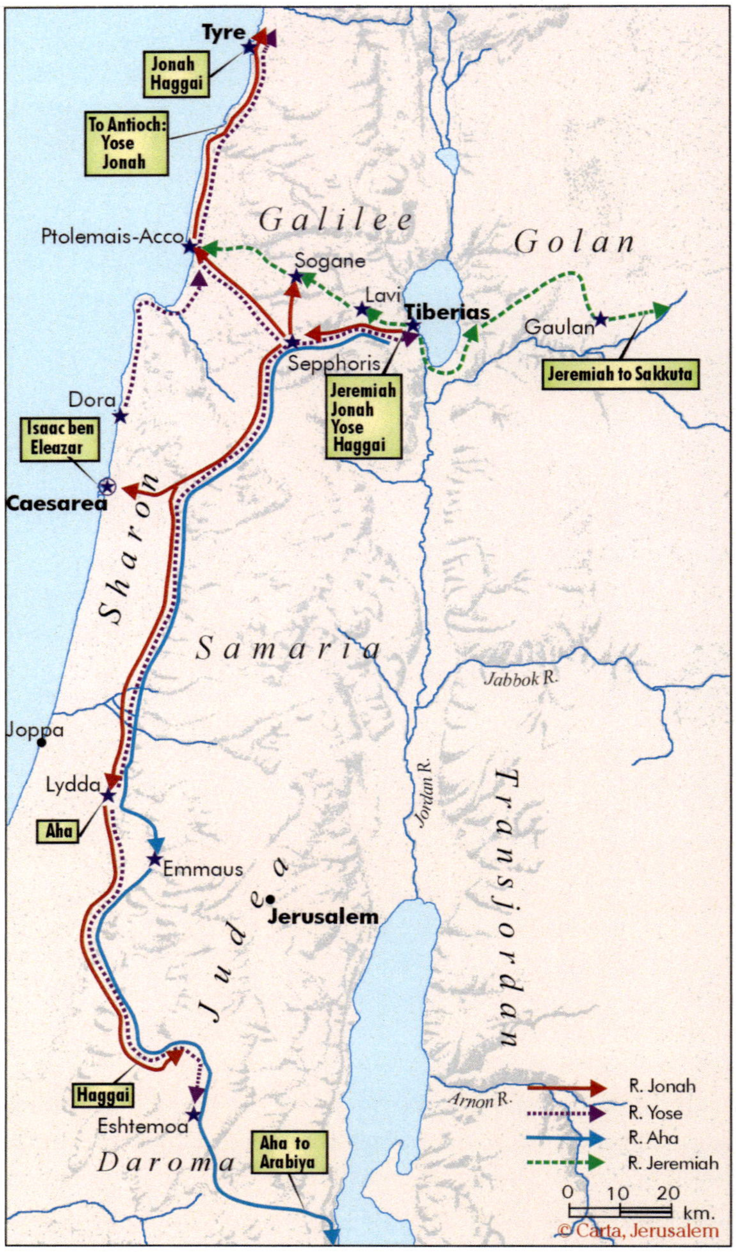

The Gallus Revolt and the Battle of Ursicinus 351 to 352

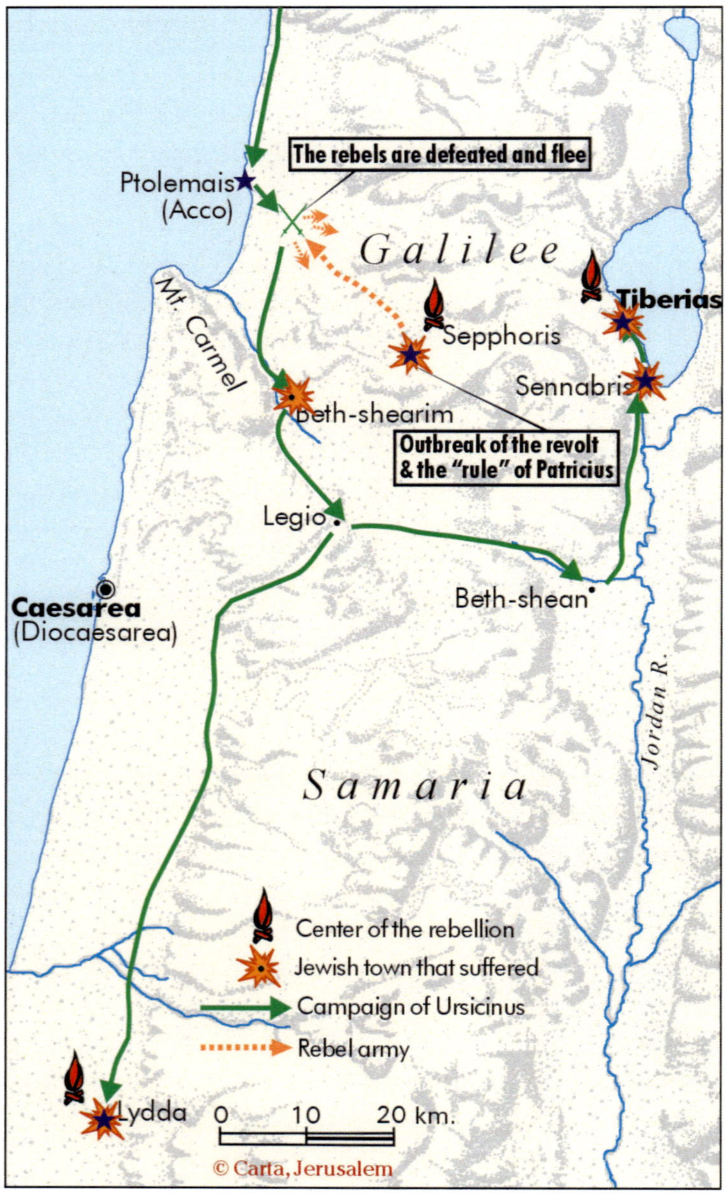

Constantius II (337–361), son of Constantine the Great, continued the religious policy of his father and harshened the anti-Jewish laws. He supported the severe economic stringencies inflicted on the Jews, mainly on those engaged in spinning and weaving. As a result a rebellion, led by a certain Patricius, broke out in Sepphoris (Diocaesarea) in 351. An assault on the Roman garrison, which was destroyed, led to their procurement of weapons, declaring Patricius king and setting up administrative rule. Constantius appointed his cousin Gallus 'Caesar of the East', who in turn dispatched an experienced commander, Ursicinus, to quell the revolt. In an encounter near Acco, the Roman army defeated the rebels and advanced to the centers of the revolt (Sepphoris, Tiberias and Lydda). On their way they destroyed the city of Beth-shearim, as evidenced by archaeological findings at the site. The *nasi* and Sanhedrin were apparently not maltreated by the Roman commander, and they continued to function for a long period. In Sepphoris, the rebels had to conceal their identity and many fled the town.

The Roman conquest was accompanied by several affronts to Jewish sentiment, such as the burning of a Torah scroll in Sennabris, and forcing the Jews to bake leavened bread during Passover for the Roman army. However, Ursicinus' attitude toward the Jews was to a large extent moderate. It is told that he treated the sages (R. Jona and R. Yose) with great respect when they came to see him in Antioch. It appears that the Jews did not suffer much from the failure of their revolt. The "destroyed" cities were soon restored and continued to populated solely by Jews. In 354, Gallus was executed, on the pretext of his ineptitude and corruption.

Roman army, 4th century, from a relief on the Arch of Constantine, Rome (photo: maggio 2005).

Julian's Attempt to Rebuild the Temple 362 TO 363

The emperor Julian (361–363), successor to Constantius II and brother of Gallus, was from his youth an enthusiastic supporter of the Hellenistic faith and a sworn enemy of Christianity. A friend of the Jews, Julian promised to rebuild the Temple and appointed a special official from among his friends to accomplish this goal. Julian's announcement aroused much excitement throughout Israel and the Diaspora. Large sums of money were raised and building materials amassed. The Jews built a temporary synagogue in Jerusalem, in one of the stoas on the Temple Mount. The Christians in Jerusalem and elsewhere were totally against the rebuilding of the Temple.

The work began in the spring of 363, when Julian crossed the Euphrates in his war against the Persians. An earthquake struck on 27 May 363, during the Temple's construction, and the building materials that were concentrated in the underground vaults of the Temple Mount caught fire. The vaults (known today as "Solomon's Stables") were located at the corner of the southern and eastern porticoes. Gases that had formed within this confined place caused an explosion, killing several laborers. Those responsible for the work stopped construction after this event, because for some time nothing was known of the fate of the emperor and his army. Julian was in fact killed on 16 June 363. His successor, Jovian, was a Christian and reinstated Constantine's policies, thereby aborting any attempt to rebuild the Temple. It is extremely doubtful if this project had the approval of the *nasi* and the Sanhedrin in the first place.

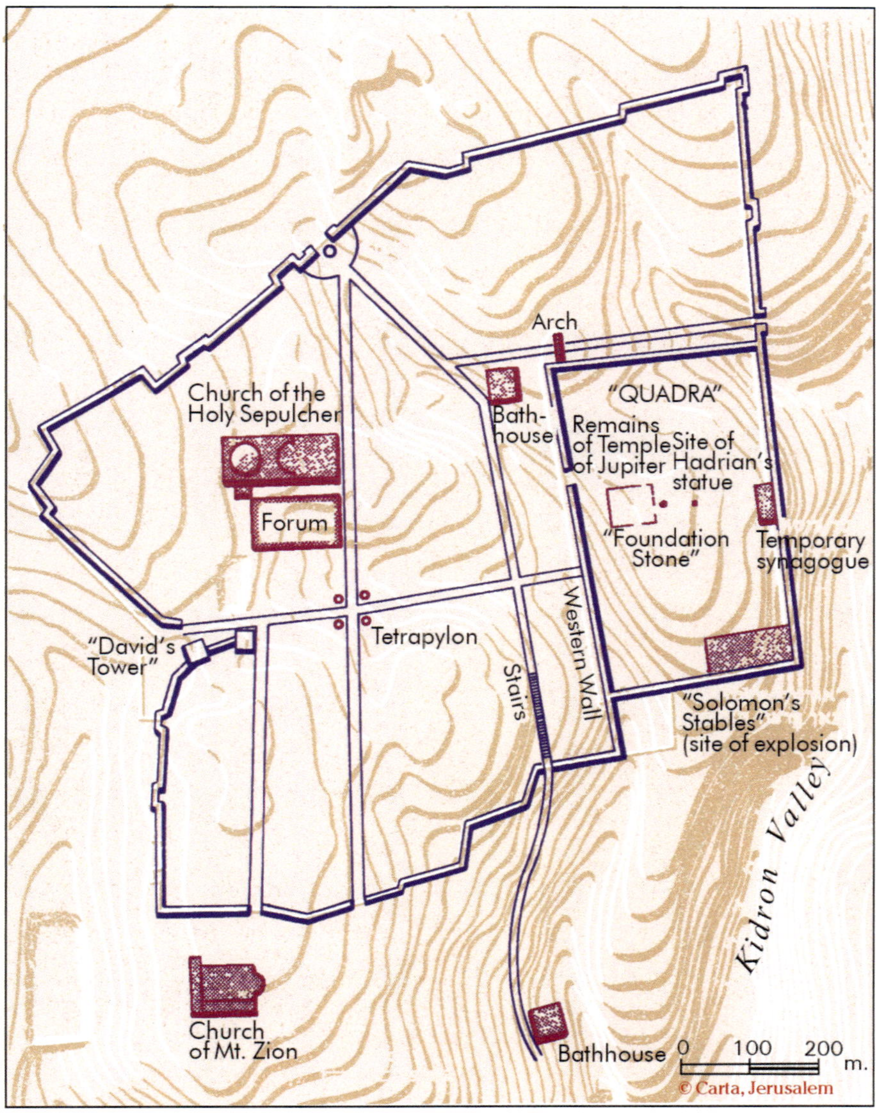

Statue of Julian the Apostate, Tongeren, Belgium (photo: Jean Housen).

The Fifth Generation of *Amoraim* 360 to 400

After the death of Emperor Julian (the Apostate) there came a long and difficult period of legislative restrictions on the Jews, which reached its zenith during the reign of Theodosius II (408–450). At that time the Jews were prohibited from holding public office and forbidden to build new synagogues. Finally, after the death of Rabban Gamaliel VI (c. 425), who left no heirs, the authorities took advantage of the situation and abolished the presidency of the Sanhedrin. The luminaries of the fifth generation of *amoraim* (360–400), among them R. Yose b. Avin and R. Mana, attended to the final editing of the Palestinian Talmud, and brought it to completion. Out of this time of distress there grew great aggadists and homilists, such as R. Phinehas bar Hama, Rabbi Tanhuma bar Abba of Naveh and R. Berechiah, who gave expression to the people's suffering and hopes.

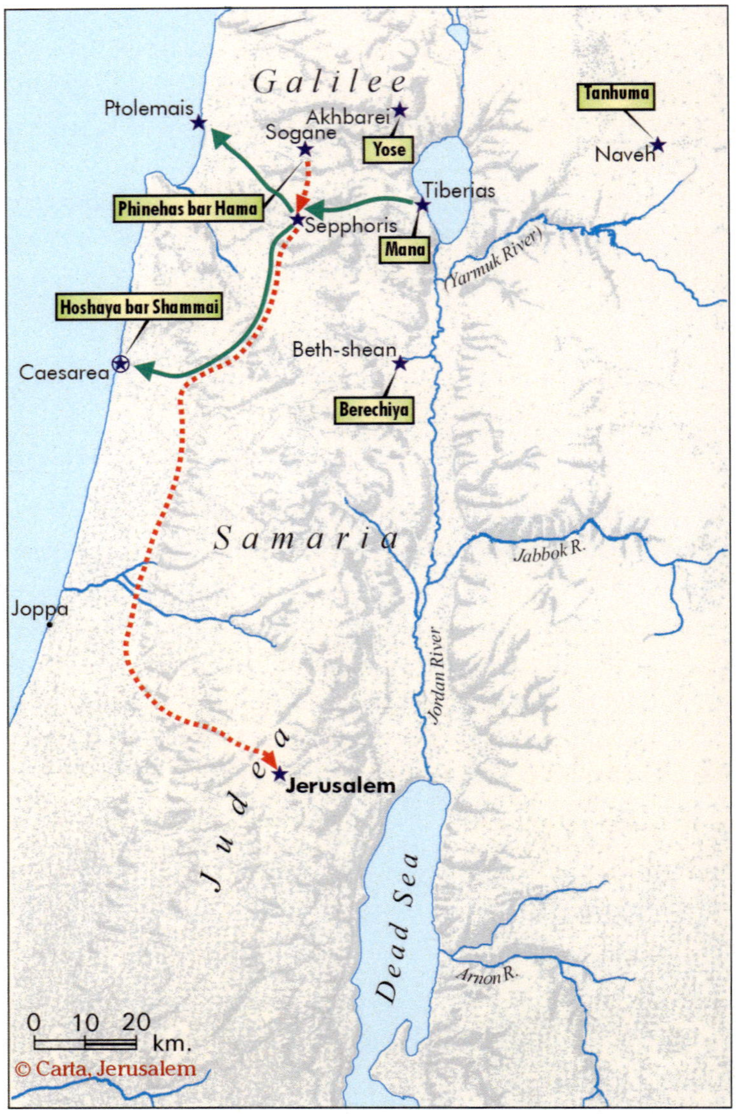

Theodosius II, Louvre Museum, Paris (in the royal collections since the 16th century).

The Jewish Settlement in the Time of Eudocia c. 450

The hardships suffered by the Jews in the Byzantine Empire, reached also the population in the Land of Israel. The decline of the Jewish population began immediately with the death of Julian. The southern settlements, between En-gedi and Gerar, were destroyed or disappeared. From that time onward, the Jewish population outside of Galilee was concentrated in the cities (apart from a few villages on the coastal plain and in the Jordan Valley). Only in Galilee did the Jews remain the majority of the population.

In the fifth century, many changes occurred that affected the conditions of the Jews in Eretz Israel. Economically, their conditions were reasonably good, since the Jews too were engaged in the economic prosperity enjoyed by the country in the Byzantine period.

The rising number of Christian pilgrims were even guided by the Jews, who knew the location of biblical sites and whose traditions were respected by the Christians. Politically, on the other hand, the situation of the Jews worsened. Between 414 and 429, the presidency had been abolished, and separate Sanhedrin courts had been established in Provinces A and B. However, this scheme

Eudocia, depicted on a mosaic in the Alexander Nevsky Cathedral, Sofia, Bulgaria (photo: Elena Chochkova).

of the authorities failed. At this time a new administrative college was established in Tiberias, headed by a *rosh perek*, who replaced the *nasi*.

Another change occurred through the intervention of the empress Eudocia, the former wife of Theodosius II, who left her husband and lived in Jerusalem until her death (460). In her time, the Jews were permitted to return to the holy city and its environs. From then on they remained in and around Jerusalem, mainly in the vicinity of Bethlehem.

We learn that R. Pinhas Bar Hama visited Jerusalem. The vitality of the Jewish population in the Land of Israel is evidenced by the number of synagogues built in the fifth and sixth centuries, in spite of prohibitions imposed by the authorities and despite attacks and waves of destruction on such places as Caesarea, Gerasa and Rabbath Moab.

Coin of Aelia Eudocia, struck 425–429 (photo: beastcoins.com).

THE AMORAIM IN BABYLONIA

The First Generation of Babylonian *Amoraim* 200 to 254

Babylonia was not affected by the troubles that beset the Roman Empire. In the first half of the third century, Ardashir (226–241), of the Sassanid Dynasty, toppled the failing Parthians and regenerated the kingdom. However, the first Sassanid king, influenced by the Zoroastrian priesthood (the "Magis"), began to restrict the rights of the Jews. Toward the end of his reign, however, and particularly in the days of his successor Shapur I, obstacles ceased to be placed in their way. The Jews set up their own law courts and developed the great yeshivas into centers for the teaching and development of talmudic law, as well as for public leadership. The exilarch in this generation, Mar Ukba (210–240), was one of the Torah sages. The head of the Nehardea community, a Jewish center for hundreds of years, was Abba bar Abba, a wealthy silk merchant who had business relations with R. Judah b. Bathyra of Nisibis. His son Samuel (d. 225) headed the yeshiva in Nehardea. He had a good relationship with the royal court, especially with King Shapur I, and supported the Persian campaigns in Asia Minor. Samuel also authored the principle that in civil matters "the law of the state is the law," that is, that Persian law must, according to *halakhah*, be obeyed by the Jews as well. This principle greatly influenced the development of *halakhah* for generations. Nehardea was also the seat of Karna, "*dayyan* (judge) of the *golah* (Diaspora)."

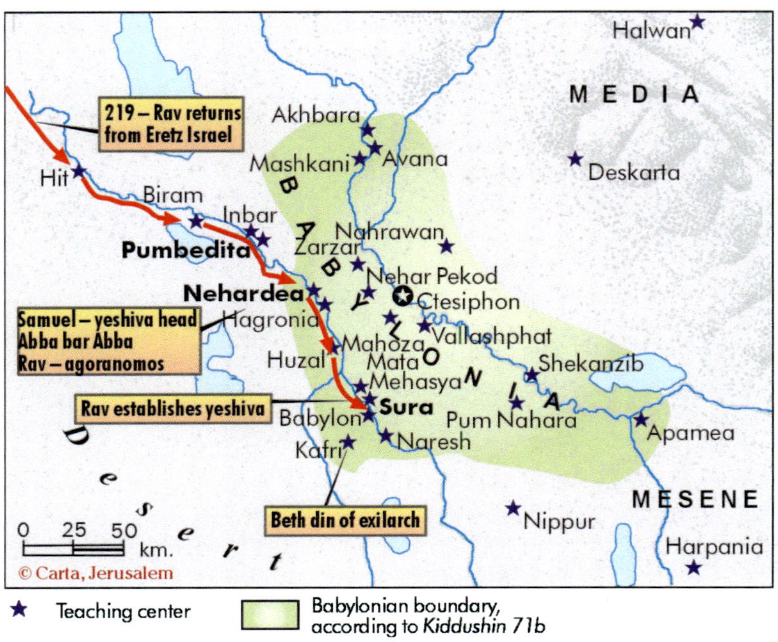

However, the decisive impetus toward the development of a Jewish spiritual center in Babylonia came from Rav (Abba Arikha), who had returned to Babylonia from Eretz Israel at the end of the days of Rabbi Judah ha-Nasi. Rav was first appointed *agoranomos* (inspector of market transactions) on behalf of the exilarch. When the position of *resh sidra* was available in Nehardea and offered to Rav, he respectfully declined the office in favor of Samuel and moved to Huzal (where R. Assi was *resh sidra*). Rav finally settled in Sura—large in population but weak in Torah—founding there a famous academy, which exercised the authority of teaching and appointing the *dayyanim* (pl. of *dayyan*) over the surrounding cities. Rav died in 247.

The Babylonian Jews were proud of their genealogy, and in the opinion of Rav, as told by R. Papa Saba, only Babylonia was in that sense "healthy" within its borders (*Kiddushin* 71b): Akhbara, Avana and Mashkani in the north, near the Tigris River, Nahrawan in the east, and Apamea in the area of the southern Tigris. Furthermore, only the areas adjacent to Babylonia—Nehavend in Media, Halwan, and the Upper Euphrates region "between the rivers"—were considered as "privileged" as Babylonia.

The Second Generation of Babylonian *Amoraim* 254 to 299

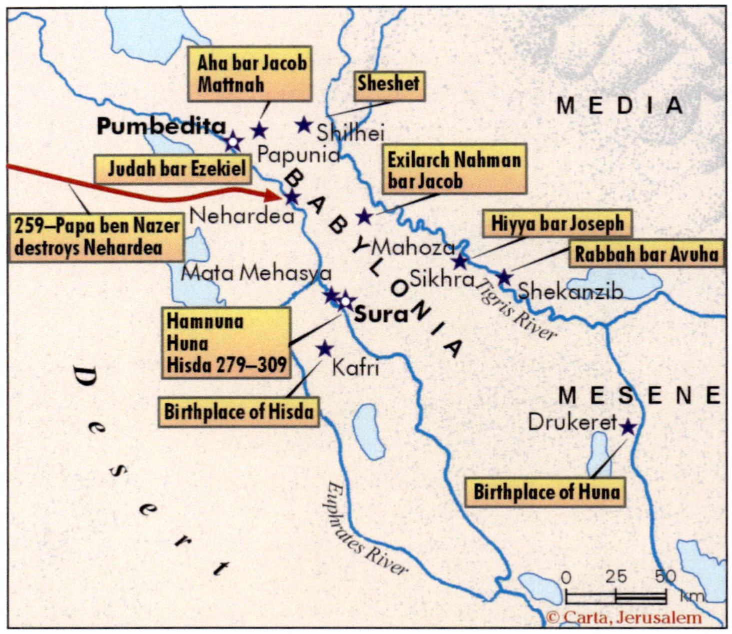

In 259 Papa ben Nazer, leading the Palmyrene troops (who then owed allegiance to Zenobia and controlled the eastern Roman Empire), destroyed Nehardea, and its sages and disciples were dispersed. In those days R. Hamnuna, and after him R. Huna, continued to preside over the Sura academy, which remained unaffected by the invasion. R. Huna, a luminary of this generation, was born in Drukeret to a distinguished but poor family. Eventually, he acquired wealth from agricultural production. During his time the Sura academy flourished and the number of its permanent students reached eight hundred.

In Sura the traditions of teaching that had drawn Rav from Eretz Israel continued. R. Huna headed the academy for about forty years. He died in 297 and his body was brought to Eretz Israel for burial. After his death R. Hisda (a native of Kafri) became head of the Sura academy until 309. R. Judah bar Ezekiel continued the traditions of Samuel and founded the Pumbedita academy, which was considered to be the continuation of Nehardea. Pumbedita was the "Babylonian" academy par excellence, and its sages, known for their intellectual acumen, shaped the ways of thought of the Babylonian Talmud.

The exilarch had his *beth din* (law court) in the city of Mahoza outside the two main centers. R. Nahman bar Jacob (d. 320) also resided there and had many pupils. R. Sheshet studied under R. Huna in Sura and later taught in Shilhei, on the river Euphrates. R. Mattnah and R. Aha bar Jacob served in Papunia, R. Hiyya bar Joseph in Sikhra (he later immigrated to Eretz Israel), and Rabbah bar Avuha in Shekanzib, Shilhei and Mahoza.

Shapur I (241–272), a friend to the sages, still ruled at the start of this generation. In the days of the six kings who succeeded him (273–310), the influence of the Magis greatly increased, and the situation of the Babylonian Jews gradually worsened, although without greatly affecting their spiritual and economic activities

Bas-relief sculpture at Naqsh-e Rostam, Iran, depicting the triumph of Shapur I over the Roman emperor Valerian (photo: Fabien Dany—www.fabiendany.com).

The Third Generation of Babylonian *Amoraim* 299 to 330

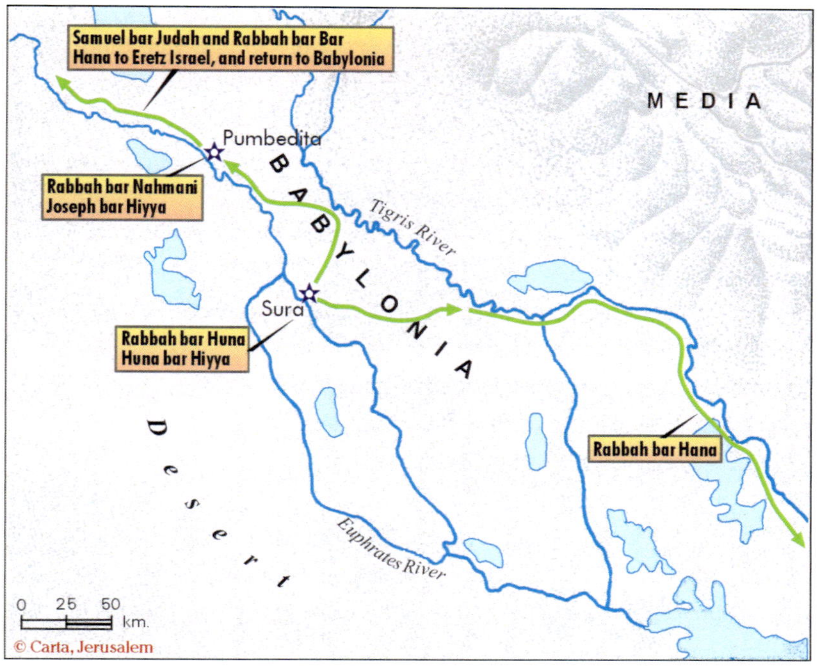

In the beginning of King Shapur II's reign (309–379) the situation of the Jews worsened, although the queen mother tended to show compassion. The Jews were declared unsuited to hold positions in the service of the state and were frequently sold into slavery for not paying their taxes on time. It reached such a point that the sages received permission to appear as non-Jews in order to survive. Rabbah bar Bar Hana even said that the Jews were better off in the Roman kingdom than under the Persian yoke, but the majority of sages thought otherwise. Many Jews were forced to abandon their lands because of the heavy taxes they had to pay: the *tasqa* and the *karga* (land tax and poll tax, respectively). As a result, in 338, the Persian authorities allotted the Jewish lands around Pumbedita to Arab settlers. Even the spiritual activities of the Jews offended the Persian regime. They complained that because of the periodic general assembly of students (who gathered for Torah study), twelve thousand people failed to pay taxes for two months, and Rabbah bar Nahmani was hounded for this until he died during his wanderings. Only after his death (320), perhaps because of the lurking dangers to the kingdom on the part of the Romans, did relations between the Persians and the Jews improve.

Despite the pressures, the centers of Torah study in Babylonia in this generation were many. Rabbah bar R. Huna headed the academy in Sura (until his death in 320), but never succeeded in filling his father's place. Characteristic of the attitude of the Jews to the Persian kingdom in the days of Shapur II was the fact that R. Huna bar Hiyya, a natural candidate to inherit R. Judah's position in Pumbedita, was disqualified when it became known that he had served as a government tax collector. He continued to teach in Sura but not as head of the yeshiva.

The outstanding sages of this generation were Rabbah bar Nahmani and R. Joseph bar Hiyya in Pumbedita. Rabbah was head of the academy for twenty-two years (until 320), followed by Rav Joseph, until 323.

In this generation the many ties between Babylonia and Eretz Israel remained intact. Thus R. Samuel bar Judah, who converted together with his father, went up to Eretz Israel and returned, bringing Torah teachings of the Palestinian sages to Babylonia. Rabbah bar Bar Hana often went up to Eretz Israel, and traveled from place to place, as he did in Babylonia. He was renowned for his numerous journeys in different lands and for the tall tales of his sea voyages and travels in the desert.

The Fourth Generation of Babylonian *Amoraim* 330 to 352

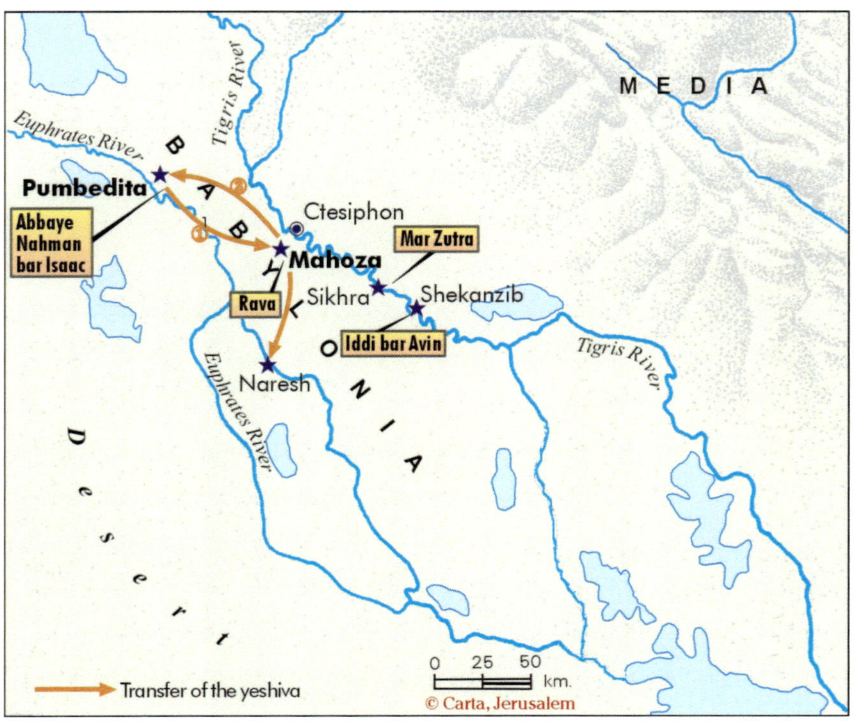

The halakhic activity was now concentrated in Pumbedita. After the death of R. Joseph there were several candidates to head the academy, among them Abbaye and Rava and R. Ze'eira. Abbaye was chosen and he presided over the academy for fourteen years (323–338), the same length of time as his successor, Rava (338–352). Under him, the academy moved to Mahoza, the home of Rava, during whose days R. Nahman bar Isaac headed the general assembly of students. Then, for four years (352–356) he headed the academy, which now returned to Pumbedita, and only one faction moved to Naresh. The sayings of Abbaye and Rava were a high point in the approach to the study of *halakhah* and talmudic law, and became known as "the disputes of Abbaye and Rava." Abbaye, an orphan who was raised by his uncle, Rabbah bar Nahmani, earned his livelihood from a parcel of land that he farmed himself. He ascribed his study and interpretation of *halakhah* to logical reasoning. Rava bar Joseph (also renowned as an aggadist) would add the practical dimension of day-to-day reality, and in the controversies between him and Abbaye, *halakhah* was usually determined according to the latter. Active outside Pumbedita were R. Iddi bar Avin, who resided in Shekanzib, and Mar Zutra, son of R. Nahman bar Jacob, who taught in Sikhra.

Toward the end of the fourth generation, the loyalty of Babylonian Jewry was put to the test when the emperor Julian, a known friend of the Jews, invaded Babylonia (363) and stormed the city of Birtha. The Jews of the city left without resistance. Julian's campaign brought about the destruction of Mahoza and Ctesiphon. However, things returned to normal after the death of the emperor and the retreat of the Roman army. Shapur II, who was highly suspicious of the Jews early in his reign, improved later on, as did the economic situation of the Babylonian Diaspora as a whole.

The ruins of Ctesphon (photo: Karl Oppolzer).

The Fifth and Sixth Generations of Babylonian *Amoraim* 352 TO 376

In the days of Kings Yezdegerd I (399–420) and Bahram V (420–438), the situation of the Jews remained stable. Yezdegerd even showed great respect toward the exilarch, R. Huna bar Nathan, despite the wrath of the Magis. However, under Yezdegerd II (438–457) and Firuz II (457–484), the Jews were persecuted, especially during the struggle against the movement for religious equality led by Mazdak. It reached the point where, in the days of King Kavadh (488–531), the exilarch Mar Zutra II headed an annual rebellion for seven years until he was taken prisoner and beheaded, and his body was suspended from a cross on the bridge at Mahoza (520). His youngest son, Mar Zutra III, escaped to Tiberias, where he was appointed to an academic position in a college (*rosh perek*). This socio-political ferment accelerated the completion of the Babylonian Talmud.

Upon the death of Rava (352), some of his students moved from Mahoza to Naresh, where R. Papa headed the yeshiva until 371, and R. Huna Bereiah de-Rav Joshua served as head of the general assembly of students. The Pumbedita academy was headed by R. Hama (until 377) and after him, R. Zevid (385). Another center was established in Pum Nahara, in which R. Kahana served, and studies were renewed in Nehardea under R. Zevid, R. Dimi, R. Hama, and others. Smaller assemblies also arose in Hagronia and in Papunia.

After the death of R. Papa, the Sura academy was revitalized and headed by R. Ashi (372–424), although it was now located at Mata Mehasya, adjacent to Sura. The exilarch also moved there, and the heads of the Pumbedita academy would often come to the Sura academy, to which they were subordinate. Here, too, the periodic general assembly of students would be arranged. R. Ashi compiled and edited the Babylonian Talmud but did not live to see its completion. He was assisted by Ravina, R. Abba and R. Hanina of Sepphoris, who transmitted many of the Torah teachings and customs of Palestinian Jewry. The sages Mar Zutra I and Ameimar taught in the *beth midrash* of R. Ashi. The efforts of all these sages brought to a conclusion the tremendous undertaking of completing the Babylonian Talmud, in which the essence of the Oral Law was crystallized and on whose basis the Jewish way of life was determined for the next fifty generations.

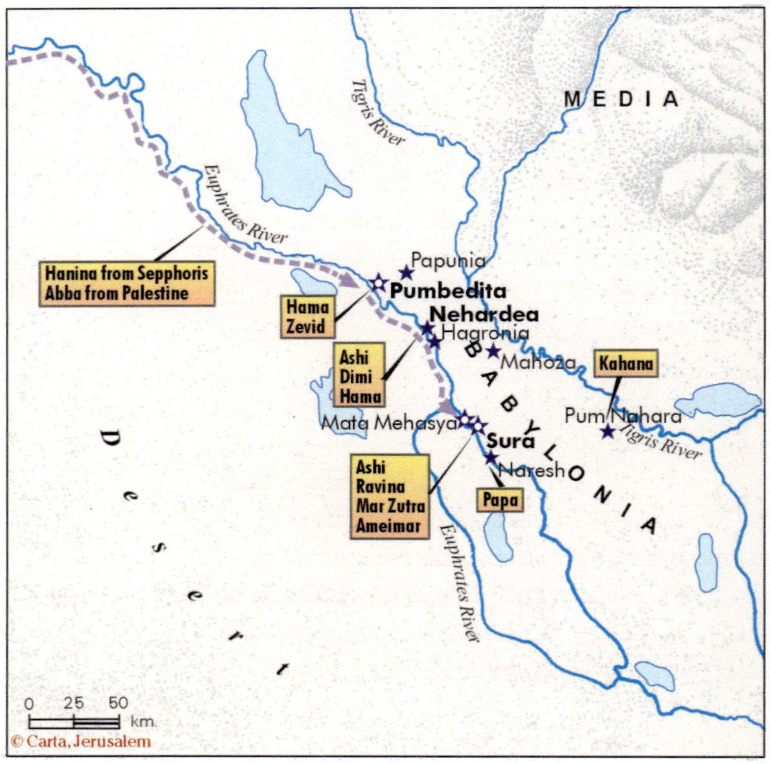

The traditional tomb of R. Ashi on Mt. Shinaan in Galilee (photo: Melamed Katz).

THE CLOSE OF THE BYZANTINE PERIOD

The Economy of Eretz Israel in the Byzantine Period

The economic situation of Palestine changed thoroughly after the time of Constantine the Great. From a small and distant province of the Roman Empire, the country became the "Holy Land" for pilgrims throughout the empire and beyond. Monks and all types of refugees settled in the land. The extensive building of churches, monasteries, shelters and hospitals, paid for by the treasury or by individual donors, brought large sums of money to the country and led to an increase in the number of workers. This spurt of building activity resulted in the arrival of craftsmen and artisans, many of whom remained and settled here. In pilgrimage centers like Jerusalem, various crafts flourished which were pilgrim-related, such as the manufacture of jewelry, the copying of Holy Scripture, shoe making, and the like. In step with the growing economic activity the population increased and that, in turn, led to the expansion of the cultivated area up to the desert frontier. Even the monasteries in the Jordan Valley, the Judean wilderness and Sinai engaged in agriculture and horticulture; pigs were also bred despite the objection of their Jewish neighbors.

Both the talmudic and non-Hebrew sources as well as archaeological findings attest to the remarkable economic prosperity of Palestine in the fourth and fifth centuries. This period of increased economic activity is characterized by our knowledge of new or rare plants, luxury products, and fruits for export apart from the basic products such as wheat. Noteworthy are the different kinds of wine that were produced from Ascalon and Gaza and exported to Egypt, Italy and as far as Gallia. The wines from the Carmel, Sharon and Ammon regions are mentioned in Jewish literary sources. Oils from Samaria were sent to Egypt. Fruits worthy of mention include dates and balsam, a product of the Jordan Valley gathered from En-gedi to Ramah (BT, *Shabbat* 26a), and figs from the coastal plain and Galilee. The cultivation of cotton began in the Jordan Valley and rice was grown in the marshy lands of the Huleh Valley. For clothing, linen was produced in Galilee and sheep were bred in Upper Galilee and the Jordan Valley. Dye manufacturing was based on the fishing of the murex "between Haifa and the ascent of Tyre" (BT, ibid.). The manufacture of fine textiles was centered in Beth-shean (Scythopolis), and replaced the textiles that were formerly imported from India and Egypt. Silk weaving was also done in the Negeb and in Galilee.

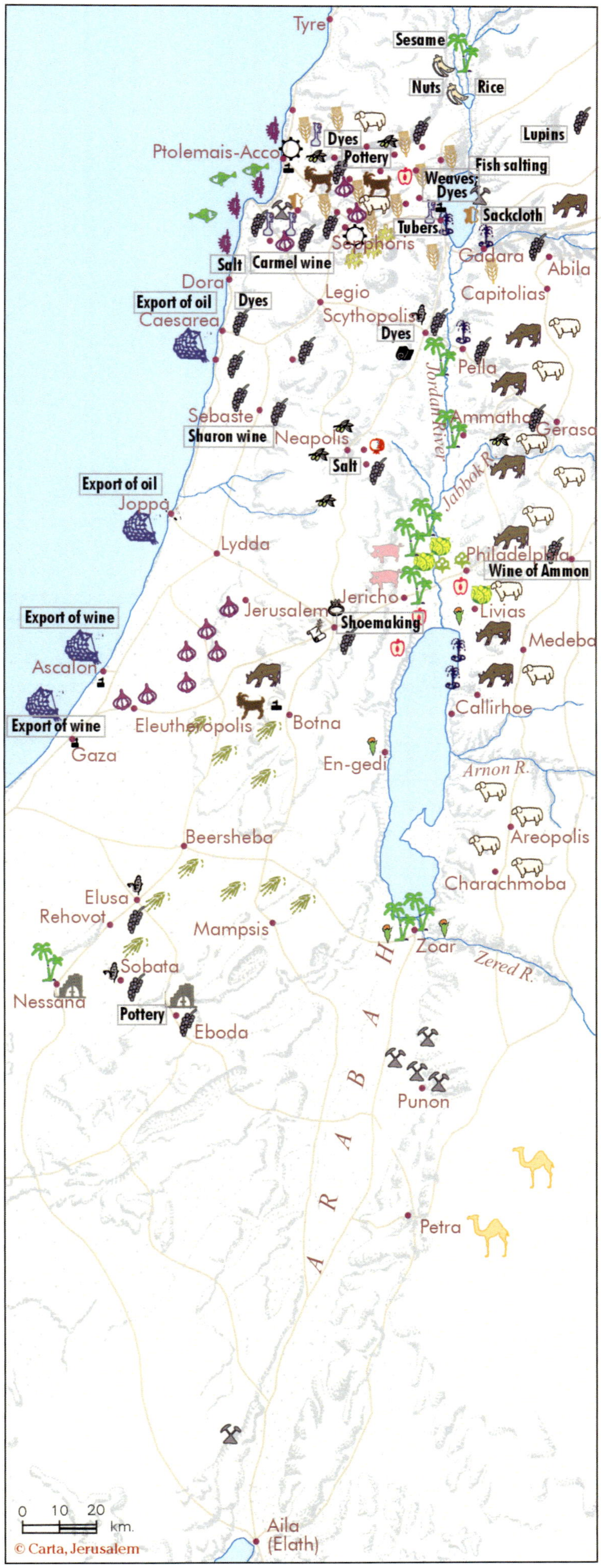

The Political Division of Eretz Israel in the Byzantine Period

The improvement in the standard of living encouraged cattle-breeding, mainly in Transjordan. Also in this period, the copper mines in the Arabah were largely exploited. These also served as an exile for undesirable Christian leaders. The hot springs, from Hammath Tiberias in the north to those of Calirrhoe and Baaru in the south, attracted many visitors both from the country and from abroad.

Economic activity during the Byzantine period reached its peak in the Negeb. In view of the increasing pressure of the Saracene Arab clans ("the eastern people") along the Transjordan border, the authorities made efforts to develop the settlements and the routes of the Negeb. These also served as a base for pilgrimage travels to Sinai. In this period, at least six cities flourished in the Negeb: Elusa, Rehovot-in-the-Negeb, Nessana, Sobata, Mampsis and Oboda. In each of these, churches, monasteries and schools were built, and factories were established, and in the southern cities located near the desert, defensive walls and fortresses were erected. The wine and oil presses in and around these cities, as well as the many irrigation facilities, such as water channels, dams and reservoirs, show that the Byzantines, in developing the Negeb, adapted methods used by the Nabateans and their predecessors, the Jews. In this way, they succeeded in maintaining cities with thousands of residents in the desolate southern parts of the country. This expansion reflected the need of the Byzantines for increasing cultivated areas. The bathhouses near the roads and inns in the cities, point to the consideration afforded the travelers in the region between the Red Sea, on the one hand, and Jerusalem and the Mediterranean ports, on the other.

The political rules laid down by Diocletian were the guiding light for all Byzantine rulers who succeeded him, from 324 until the conquests of the Persians (614) and the Arabs (640). The separation of military and state was strictly observed. The division of the old provinces into smaller units finally reached even *Palaestina*, one of the less important areas of the Byzantine Empire. In about 358 the entire southern part of the province (enlarged under Diocletian), along with the *limes* (but not the western estates, namely, Sycomazon, the Constantinian estate and the estate of Gerar)—i.e., the Negeb and southern Transjordan—became a special province called *Palaestina Salutaris* ("Palestine of Salvation"), with its capital at Petra.

In about 425 the process of decentralization was completed by dividing the rest of the country into two parts: *Palaestina* A (*Prima*), with its capital at Caesarea, formerly the capital of the whole province; and *Palaestina* B (*Secunda*), whose capital was the large "city of weavers," Beth-shean (Scythopolis). *Palaestina* A included the coastal cities and estates therein, the Judean Hills and the Hills of Ephraim, the Jordan Valley, and "Jewish Transjordan" (formerly Perea). *Palaestina* B included the Esdraelon Valley, Lower and Upper Galilee, the cities of Pella, Gadara, Hippus (Sussita), Capitolias and Abila, and also the

Golan. This province thus included most of the remaining Jewish settlement in Eretz Israel. With the establishment of *Palaestina* A and B, the authorities changed the name *Palaestina Salutaris* to *Palaestina* C (*Tertia*). These names remained in place until the end of the Byzantine period.

The three provinces were headed by governors of varying ranks (the most senior being the governor of Caesarea). The provinces themselves were divided into urban areas and estates or districts with no urban structure. In the Byzantine period, however, there was already no great significance to an independent urban regime, the cities being administrative units. The decentralization process affected the urban areas as well. The Gaza region was divided in three—Gaza, Constantia (Maiumas Gaza) and Anthedon—as was the Ascalon area: Ascalon, Maiumas Ascalon and Diocletianopolis. Azotus (Ashdod) now became two cities: inland Azotus lost its importance, and Azotus-on-Sea (Azotus Paralios) became a large city, as did Jamnia (Jabneh). A separate unit, Tricomias, may have been formed in the area of Eleutheropolis. Long before this time, Ono had been separated from Lydda Diospolis. The Naim district was separated from Sepphoris after the latter was separated from the Hellenopolis district. These changes completed the urbanization process in the Byzantine period.

One of three Byzantine basilicas found at Pella (photo: Ben Churcher, Pella Project, University of Sydney, Australia).

Collonaded street, Byzantine period, at Scythopolis (photo: Carole Raddato, Frankfurt, Germany).

Remains of the Byzantine quarter at Oboda (photo: Mboesch).

The Synagogue Remains in Eretz Israel

The remains of synagogues spread all over the area of Jewish settlement in Eretz Israel from the time of the destruction of the Temple onward are the most substantial expression of the vitality of the Jewish population of the country. These synagogues may be divided into three types (not including the remains of the most ancient synagogue at Masada and the inscription found in Jerusalem which attests to the existence of a synagogue there).

The ancient type, dating from the second to third centuries CE, is found mainly in Galilee. It is characterized by a decorated facade with three openings oriented toward Jerusalem; the walls were lined with benches, where worshippers sat facing each other so as not to have their backs toward Jerusalem; only the elders and the cantor (*hazzan*) who prayed at the ark of the law faced the Holy City. The inner hall was divided lengthwise by two rows of columns and by one row across; benches lined the walls apart from the entrance. A gallery rested on the columns. The building was paved with flagstones and the walls were decorated in reliefs, sometimes with animal or human images. Most prominent is the frieze which adorned the gallery. In front of the synagogue there was a courtyard or porch.

The entrance on the side facing Jerusalem was not convenient, since the visitors had to turn back or to the side in order that they pray in the direction of the Holy City. This brought about a few architectural attempts which characterise the transition type of the fourth and fifth centuries. In buildings of this type, a permanent structure for the Holy Ark has been added on the side facing Jerusalem which contained a unique room. Occasionally, synagogues were built in the form of a broad room with entrances on the short sides. In this period the mosaic floors were introduced. Belonging to the transition period, it is difficult to find a common denominator for these synagogues.

The later type (fifth to eighth centuries) of synagogues had a newly designed form. The buildings were in the form of a basilica – a long hall divided by two colonades along its length, forming three parts. The galleries were above the colonades. The semicircular apse faced Jerusalem, with the entrance on the opposite side. The Holy Ark was placed in the apse which stood on a platform and in front of it was the praying area which sometimes was deeper than the floor of the house ('calling God from the depths'). A grid with columns separated the ape from the hall. The floor of the hall was decorated with colorful mosaics. The outside of the buildings was simple and not decorated according to the dictates of the antagonistic Byzantine authorities. A narthex was usually added to the synagogue, as well as a court with a well in its center, and various rooms which served as dwellings, hospital and study rooms.

The Samaritan synagogues did not differ from those of the Jews, but for their direction. They faced Mount Gerizim. Their decorations differed and their inscriptions were written in the Samaritan script (an off-shoot of the ancient Hebrew script). In many places only scanty remains survived; and in some cases only references remained in Jewish or foreign literary sources.

(above) Facade and porch of the synagogue at Bar'am (Kefar Bir'am), 3rd century (photo: Ori~ via Wikimedia Commons).

(below) Mosaic floor of the nave in the Beth Alpha synagogue, 6th century (photo: Zxc0505, via Wikimedia Commons).

Gold glass decorated with Jewish symbols, from Rome.

The Jewish Diaspora in the Fifth Century

Theodosius I (383–395) was the last Roman emperor to rule over the whole empire. Upon his death the empire was divided between his sons, Arcadeus (Emperor of the East) and Honorius (Emperor of the West). This division remained permanent ever after. The Romans stood their ground in the east, but within three generations the western empire collapsed under the pressure of various invading German tribes. The Ostrogoths ruled in Italy, the Franks and the Burgundians in northern France, the Visigoths in southern France and Spain, and the Vandals in Africa. Thus the Jewish Diaspora in the west came under many rulers, being treated moderately well by some and persecuted by others.

By the end of the ancient period the Jewish communities had spread in all directions—northward (to the river Rhine), westward (to France) and southward. The communities multiplied particularly in the south of Spain, despite their harsh treatment by the Visigoth kings, who abandoned Arian beliefs in 589. Communities also multiplied in Italy in the fourth and fifth centuries, some even finding protection in the shadow of the papacy, whose influence was great in the central and southern parts of the country.

In the Byzantine Empire, with the death of Julian and particularly in the time of Theodosius II (408–450), there was a strong anti-Jewis orientation. Christian monks roused the masses to attack synagogue Although the authorities disapproved of such violent acts, they forbac the establishment of new synagogues. However, they did not as y interfere with Jewish customs or make it too difficult for the Jews earn their livelihood. Nevertheless, the situation of the Jews in tl Byzantine Empire was rather miserable. The pressure increased eve more in the days of Emperor Justinian (525–565) and his successor It is therefore easy to understand why the Jews turned their backs c the repressive regime and sought allies outside the empire.

The Babylonian Diaspora presented an entirely different picture; those days it reached its height both materially and spiritually. The kin of the Sassanid Dynasty treated the Jews benevolently. The exilarc descended from King David, stood at the head of Babylonian Jewr He oversaw the wide network of administrative and legal institutio spread throughout Babylonia, in the numerous cities inhabited by tl Jews. The majority of Babylonian Jews engaged in agriculture and few in commerce and industry. The generations of Babylonian *amorai* attest to the spiritual eminence of Babylonian Jewry.

An oil lamp from Palestine.

OTHER TITLES IN THE UNDERSTANDING SERIES

Baruch Sarel

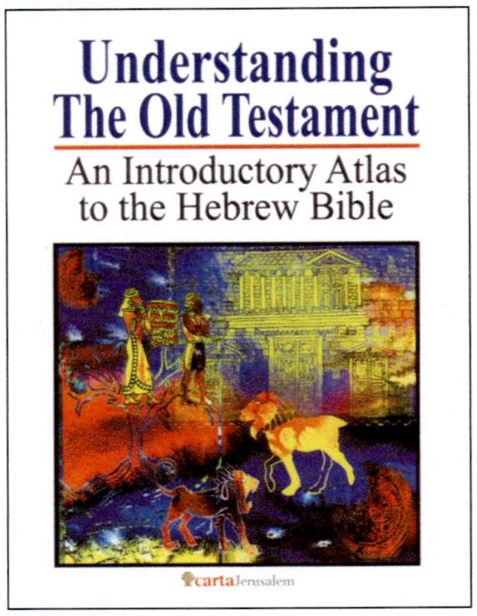

Paul H. Wright

Menashe Har-El & Paul H. Wright

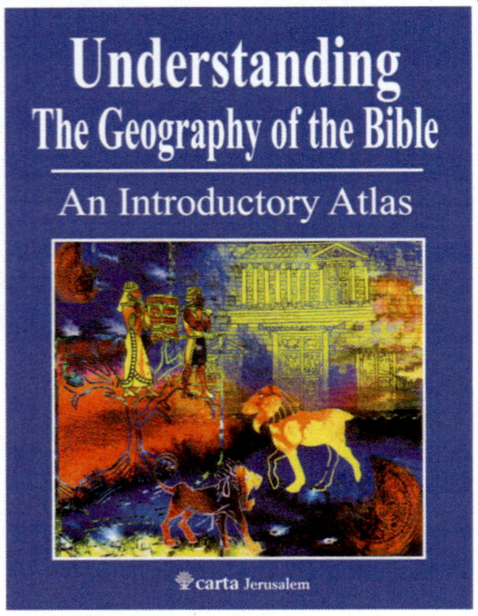

Paul H. Wright

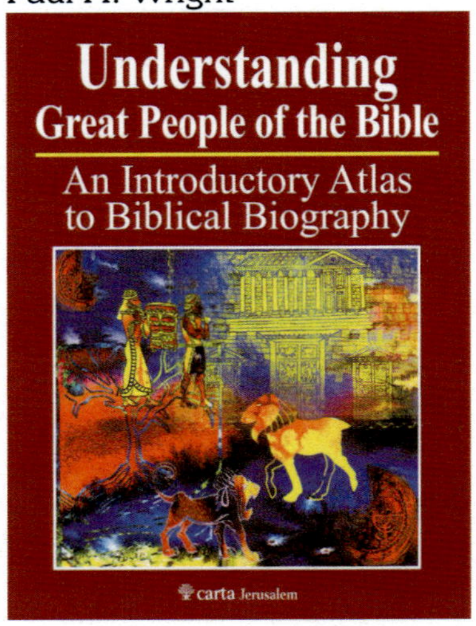

Paul H. Wright

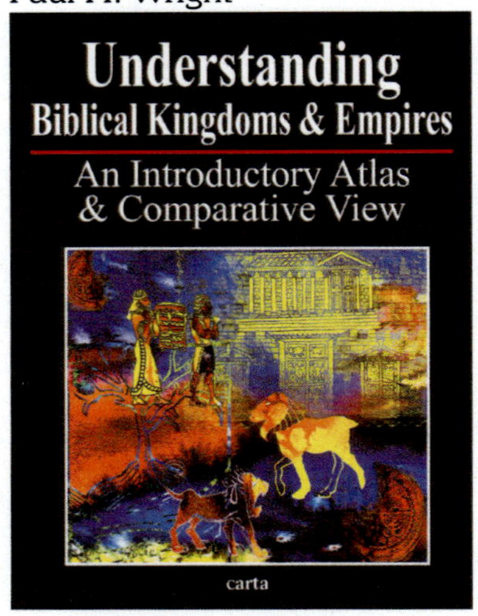

Paul H. Wright

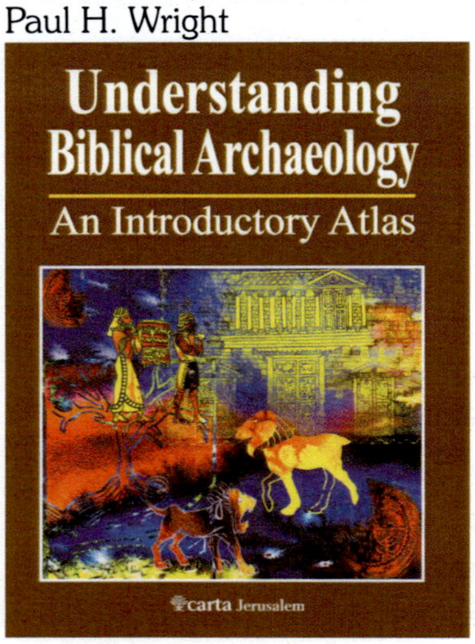

Michael Avi-Yonah & R. Steven Notley

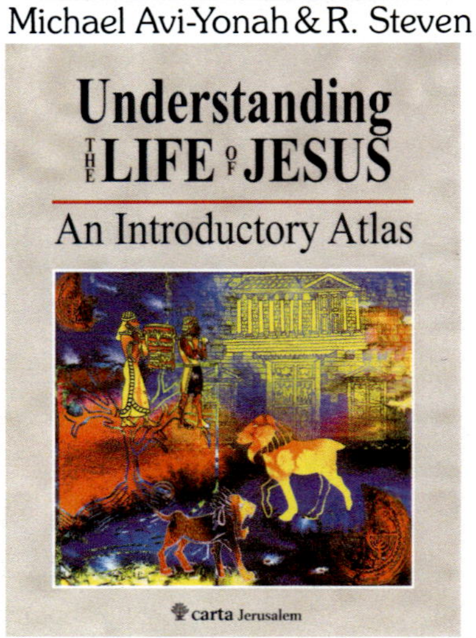

Shelley Wachsmann

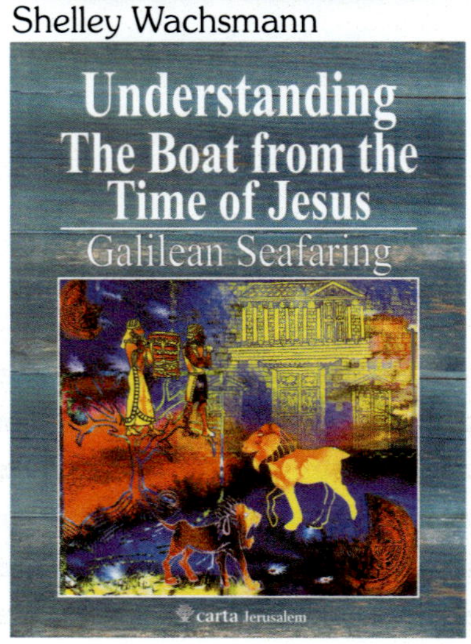

Ada Yardeni

Franklin H. Littell

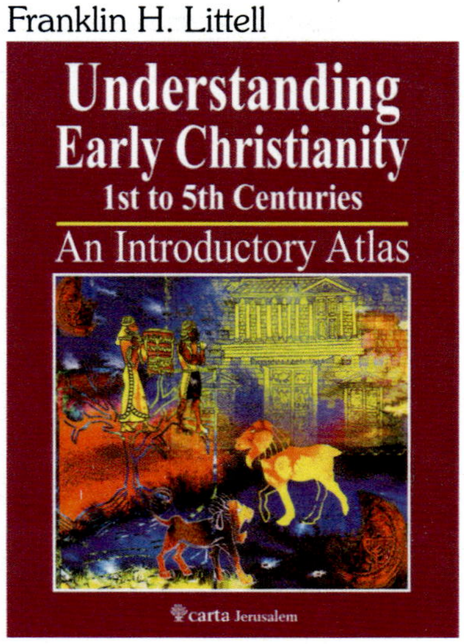

LOOK OUT FOR NEW TITLES @

carta-jerusalem.com